Illustrative
Mathematics®
LEARN MATH FOR LIFE

Kendall Hunt

GRADE 3
Units

5 | 6

Student Edition Units 5-6

Certified by Illustrative Mathematics®

ISBN 978-1-7924-6352-5

K5_v1

20211204

GRADE 3
Unit

5

Student Edition Units 5-6

Certified by Illustrative Mathematics®

Section A: Introduction to Fractions

Lesson 1: Name the Parts

- Let's name parts of a whole.

Warm-up: Which One Doesn't Belong: Shapes with Parts

Which one doesn't belong?

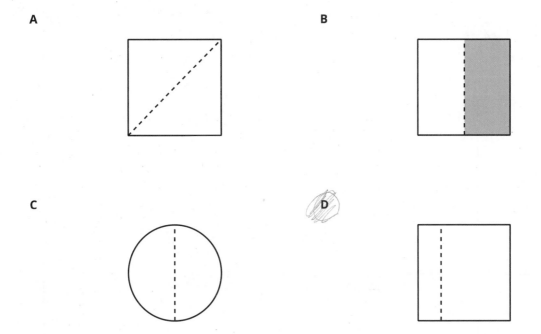

A

B

C

D

1.1: Card Sort: Partitions

Your teacher will give you a set of cards that show some shapes that are partitioned.

Sort the cards into 2 categories of your choosing. Be prepared to explain the meaning of your categories.

A

B

C

D

E

F

G

H

I

J

K

L

iM KH

1.2: Fold and Name

Fold each rectangle your teacher gives you into 3, 6, 4, or 8 equal parts. Draw lines where you folded to partition the rectangles. Be prepared to share how you folded your shapes.

Lesson 2: Name Parts as Fractions

- Let's use fractions to describe parts.

Warm-up: Which One Doesn't Belong: Shaded Parts

Which one doesn't belong?

A

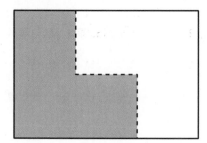

B

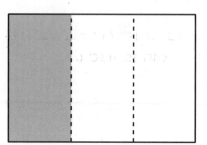

C

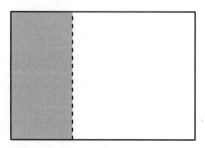

D

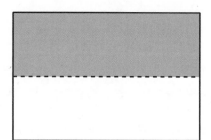

2.1: Partition the Strips

Your teacher will give you some paper strips. Each strip represents 1.

Fold each strip so that the parts represent one of the following fractions. Use one strip for each fraction.

- halves
- fourths
- eighths
- thirds
- sixths

When you finish folding, trace your folding lines with a pencil and then label each part with the correct fraction.

2.2: Partition, Shade, Trade

1. Partition each rectangle into halves, thirds, fourths, sixths, and eighths. Then label each part with the correct fraction.

halves

$\frac{1}{2}$	$\frac{1}{2}$

sixths

$\frac{1}{6}$	$\frac{1}{6}$	$\frac{1}{6}$	$\frac{1}{6}$	$\frac{1}{6}$	$\frac{1}{6}$

thirds

$\frac{1}{3}$	$\frac{1}{3}$	$\frac{1}{3}$

eighths

$\frac{1}{8}$	$\frac{1}{8}$	$\frac{1}{8}$	$\frac{1}{8}$	$\frac{1}{8}$	$\frac{1}{8}$	$\frac{1}{8}$

fourths

$\frac{1}{4}$	$\frac{1}{4}$	$\frac{1}{4}$	$\frac{1}{4}$

2.   a. Partition the rectangle into equal-sized parts. Shade one of the parts.

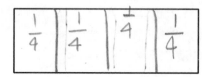

   b. Trade rectangles with a partner. If the whole rectangle is 1, what number represents the shaded part? Explain your reasoning.

$\frac{1}{16}$ because she made 16 equl parts and one is shaded in.

iM KH

Lesson 3: Non-unit Fractions

- Let's learn about non-unit fractions.

Warm-up: Notice and Wonder: More than One Part

What do you notice? What do you wonder?

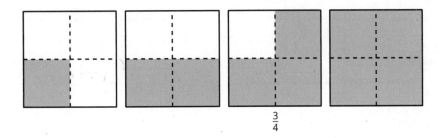

3.1: Write and Read Fractions

Each shape in each row of the table represents 1. Use the shaded parts to complete the missing information in the table. Be prepared to explain your reasoning.

	number of shaded parts	size of each part	word name for the shaded parts	number name for the shaded parts
	1	$\frac{1}{4}$	one-fourth	$\frac{1}{4}$
	3	$\frac{1}{4}$	three-fourths	$\frac{3}{4}$
	4	$\frac{1}{4}$	four-fourths	1
	2	$\frac{1}{3}$	two-thirds	$\frac{2}{3}$
	3	$\frac{1}{8}$	three-eighths	$\frac{3}{8}$

iM KH

	number of shaded parts	size of each part	word name for the shaded parts	number name for the shaded parts
	4	$\frac{1}{6}$	one-sixth	$\frac{4}{6}$
	6	$\frac{1}{4}$	one and two-fourths	$1\frac{2}{4}$
	7	$\frac{1}{6}$	One and One-sixth	$1\frac{1}{6}$

3.2: Fraction Match

Your teacher will give you a set of cards for playing Fraction Match. Two cards are a match if one is a diagram and the other a number, but they have the same value.

1. To play Fraction Match:

   ○ Arrange the cards face down in an array.

   ○ Take turns choosing 2 cards. If the cards match, keep them and go again. If not, return them to where they were, face down. You can't keep more than 2 matches on each turn.

   ○ After all the matches have been found, the player with the most cards wins.

2. Use the cards your teacher gives you to create 4 new pairs of cards to add to the set.

3. Play another round of Fraction Match using all the cards.

Lesson 4: Build Fractions from Unit Fractions

- Let's build other fractions from unit fractions.

Warm-up: Number Talk: 3 and Another Factor

Find the value of each expression mentally.

- 3×3

- 7×3

- 10×3

- 3×17

4.1: Introduce Secret Fractions

The goal of the game is to be the first to build 2 secret fractions with unit fractions.

1. Make two stacks: one for secret fractions and one for unit fractions. Place all cards face down.

2. Each player draws 2 secret fraction cards. These are the fractions you are trying to make with your unit fractions.

3. On your turn, you can make one of these moves:

   ○ Pick up 1 unit fraction card.

   ○ Trade both of your secret fractions for 2 new secret fractions from the stack.

4. When you have enough unit fractions to make one of your secret fractions, shade your gameboard to represent your secret fraction. Then, pick a new secret fraction.

5. The first player to make 2 secret fractions wins.

Gameboard

1 whole							
$\frac{1}{2}$				$\frac{1}{2}$			
$\frac{1}{3}$		$\frac{1}{3}$			$\frac{1}{3}$		
$\frac{1}{4}$		$\frac{1}{4}$		$\frac{1}{4}$		$\frac{1}{4}$	
$\frac{1}{6}$	$\frac{1}{6}$	$\frac{1}{6}$	$\frac{1}{6}$	$\frac{1}{6}$	$\frac{1}{6}$		
$\frac{1}{8}$	$\frac{1}{8}$	$\frac{1}{8}$	$\frac{1}{8}$	$\frac{1}{8}$	$\frac{1}{8}$	$\frac{1}{8}$	$\frac{1}{8}$
1 whole							
$\frac{1}{2}$				$\frac{1}{2}$			
$\frac{1}{3}$		$\frac{1}{3}$			$\frac{1}{3}$		
$\frac{1}{4}$		$\frac{1}{4}$		$\frac{1}{4}$		$\frac{1}{4}$	
$\frac{1}{6}$	$\frac{1}{6}$	$\frac{1}{6}$	$\frac{1}{6}$	$\frac{1}{6}$	$\frac{1}{6}$		
$\frac{1}{8}$	$\frac{1}{8}$	$\frac{1}{8}$	$\frac{1}{8}$	$\frac{1}{8}$	$\frac{1}{8}$	$\frac{1}{8}$	$\frac{1}{8}$

iM KH

4.2: Represent Fraction Situations

Here are four situations about playing Pilolo and four diagrams. Each diagram represents the length of a street where the game is played.

Represent each situation on a diagram. Be prepared to explain your reasoning.

1. A student walks $\frac{4}{8}$ the length of the street and hides a rock.

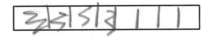

2. A student walks $\frac{2}{3}$ the length of the street and hides a penny.

3. A student walks $\frac{3}{4}$ the length of the street and hides a stick.

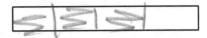

4. A student walks $\frac{5}{6}$ the length of the street and hides a penny.

5. This diagram represents the location of a hidden stick.

About what fraction of the length of the street did the student walk to hide it? Be prepared to explain how you know.

$\frac{1}{8}$ be cause it is the same lenghth of it

Section A Summary

In this section, we learned how to partition shapes into halves, thirds, fourths, sixths, and eighths, and how to describe each of those parts in words and using a number.

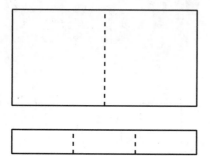
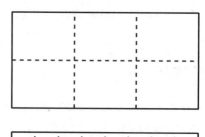

The numbers we use to describe these equal-sized parts are **fractions**.

A fraction like $\frac{1}{4}$ is read "one-fourth" because it represents one of the 4 equal parts in a whole.

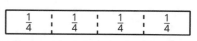

A fraction like $\frac{3}{4}$ is read "three-fourths" because it represents 3 parts that are each one-fourth or $\frac{1}{4}$ in size.

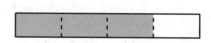

Fractions that refer to only one of the equal parts in a whole— like $\frac{1}{2}$, $\frac{1}{3}$, $\frac{1}{8}$ —are called **unit fractions**.

We learned that the bottom part of the fraction tells us how many equal parts we partitioned the whole into. The top part of the fraction tells us how many of the equal parts are being described.

iM KH

Section A Practice Problems

1. Pre-unit

Partition the rectangle into 10 equal squares.

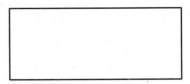

2. Pre-unit

Here are two equal-size squares. A part of each square is shaded.

Is the same amount of each square shaded? Explain or show your reasoning.

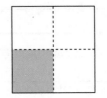 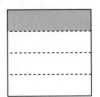

3. Pre-unit

0   100

a. Label the tick marks on the number line.

b. Locate and label 45 and 62 on the number line.

4. Pre-unit

Fill in each blank with < or > to compare the numbers.

a. 718 _____ 817

b. 106 _____ 89

c. 806 _____ 809

5. Partition the rectangle into 6 equal parts.

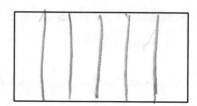

(From Unit 5, Lesson 1.)

6.   a. What fraction of the rectangle is shaded?

$\frac{1}{6}$

b. Partition the rectangle into 8 equal parts.

What fraction of the whole rectangle does each part represent?

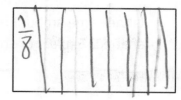

$\frac{1}{8}$

(From Unit 5, Lesson 2.)

7.   a. What fraction of the rectangle is shaded? Explain how you know.

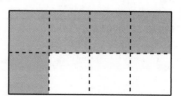

$\frac{5}{8}$ because 5 out of 8 is shaded

b. Shade $\frac{4}{6}$ of the rectangle.

(From Unit 5, Lesson 3.)

8. Jada walks across the street at a stoplight $\frac{5}{6}$ of her way from home to school. Represent the situation on the fraction strip. Explain your reasoning.

it represents it because 5 out of the 6 is shaded

(From Unit 5, Lesson 4.)

9. **Exploration**

Write a situation represented by the diagram. Explain why the diagram represents your situation.

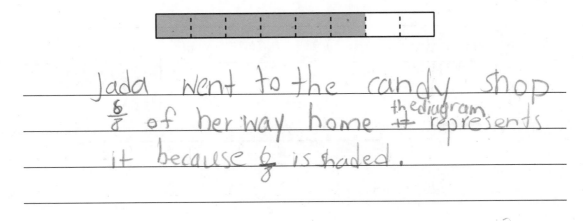

Jada went to the candy shop $\frac{6}{8}$ of her way home the diagram represents it because $\frac{6}{8}$ is shaded.

10. **Exploration**

Lin shaded part of some fraction strips. What fraction did she shade in each one? Explain how you know.

a.

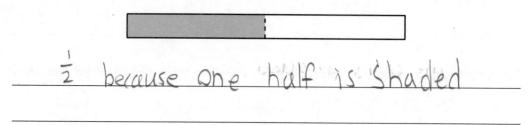

$\frac{1}{2}$ because one half is shaded

b.

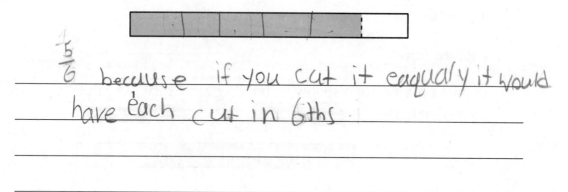

$\frac{5}{6}$ because if you cut it eaqualy it would have each cut in 6ths.

c.

$\frac{1}{3}$ is shaded because if you count this, as $\frac{1}{3}$ than $\frac{1}{3}$ would be shaded

iM KH

Section B: Fractions on the Number Line
Lesson 5: To the Number Line

- Let's learn about fractions on the number line.

Warm-up: Notice and Wonder: Two Number Lines

What do you notice? What do you wonder?

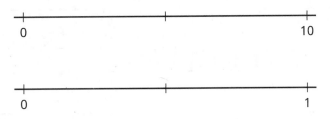

5.1: Card Sort: Number Lines

Your teacher will give you a set of cards that show number lines. Sort the cards into categories of your choosing. Be prepared to explain the meaning of your categories.

A

B

C

D

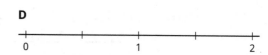

E

F

G

H

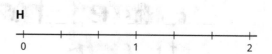

I

iM KH

5.2: Fold and Label the Number Line

1. Andre and Clare are talking about how to label fractions on the number line.
   Andre says $\frac{1}{2}$ can be labeled like this:

   Clare says $\frac{1}{2}$ can be labeled like this:

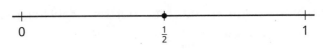

   How could each student's labeling make sense?

   Andre's method is he folded it into
   halfs and fold the halfs into halfs
   Claire's metod is just folding it
   in half

2. Your teacher will give you a set of number lines. Cut your number lines apart so that you can fold each one.

   As you fold, discuss your strategies with your partner.

   a. Fold one of the number lines into halves. Draw tick marks to show the halves. Label the number $\frac{1}{2}$.

   b. Fold one of the number lines into thirds. Draw tick marks to show the thirds. Label the number $\frac{1}{3}$.

   c. Fold one of the number lines into fourths. Draw tick marks to show the fourths. Label the number $\frac{1}{4}$.

   d. Fold one of the number lines into sixths. Draw tick marks to show the sixths. Label the number $\frac{1}{6}$.

   e. Fold one of the number lines into eighths. Draw tick marks to show the eighths. Label the number $\frac{1}{8}$.

iM KH

Lesson 6: Locate Unit Fractions on the Number Line

- Let's partition the number line to locate unit fractions.

Warm-up: Which One Doesn't Belong: Fraction Details

Which one doesn't belong?

A

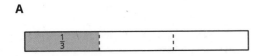

B

C

D

6.1: Partition Fourths

Three students are partitioning a number line into fourths. Their work is shown.

Clare's number line:

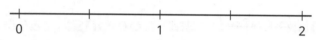

Andre's number line:

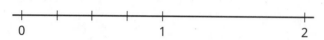

Diego's number line:

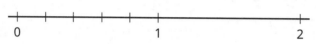

Whose partitioning makes the most sense to you? Explain your reasoning.

Andre's because he used half the number line but it is split in fourths in half to make forth's

iM KH

6.2: Unit Fractions on the Number Line

Partition each number line. Locate and label each fraction.

1. $\frac{1}{4}$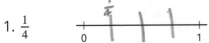

2. $\frac{1}{8}$

3. $\frac{1}{3}$

4. $\frac{1}{6}$

5. $\frac{1}{2}$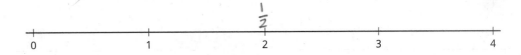

6. $\frac{1}{4}$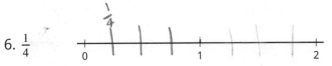

7. $\frac{1}{8}$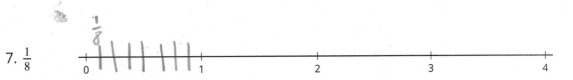

8. $\frac{1}{3}$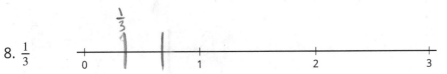

9. $\frac{1}{6}$

Lesson 7: Non-unit Fractions on the Number Line

- Let's locate non-unit fractions on the number line.

7.2: Fractions on the Number Line

1. Locate and label $\frac{3}{4}$ and $\frac{6}{4}$.

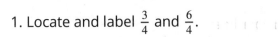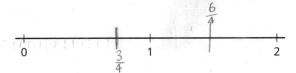

2. Locate and label $\frac{7}{8}$ and $\frac{12}{8}$.

3. Locate and label $\frac{2}{3}$ and $\frac{4}{3}$.

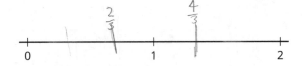

4. Locate and label $\frac{2}{6}$ and $\frac{7}{6}$.

5. How did you partition the number line when you were locating the numbers $\frac{7}{8}$ and $\frac{12}{8}$? Explain your reasoning.

I first put 8 tick marks on each 0-1 1-2 then I counted 7 tick marks and labled $\frac{7}{8}$ then I counted 5 more to make $\frac{12}{8}$.

6. What patterns did you notice in the fractions you located?

it was easyer to make the same number of tick mark as the denominator.

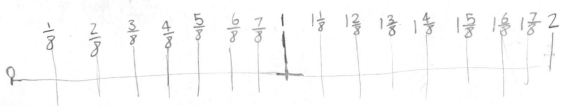

7.3: What's the Fraction?

1. Partition the number line into any number of equal-size parts. Locate and mark, but don't label, a fraction of your choice.

2. Trade number lines with a partner.

   a. How did your partner partition their number line?

   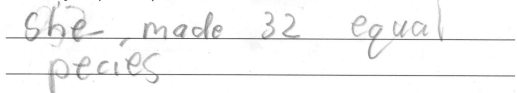

   She made 32 equal pecies

   b. What number did your partner mark on their number line? Explain your reasoning.

   _____

   _____

If you have time, play the game again.

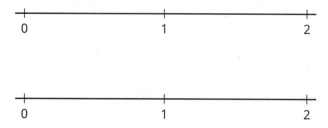

iM KH

Lesson 8: Fractions and Whole Numbers

- Let's work with fractions and whole numbers on the number line.

Warm-up: Number Talk: Divide by 4

Find the value of each expression mentally.

- $12 \div 4 = 3$

- $24 \div 4 = 6$

- $60 \div 4 = 15$

- $72 \div 4 = 18$

8.1: Fractions Located at Whole Numbers

1. Locate and label your assigned fractions on the number line. Be prepared to explain your reasoning.

0   1   2   3   4   5

a. $\frac{1}{2}, \frac{2}{2}, \frac{3}{2}, \frac{4}{2}, \frac{5}{2}, \frac{6}{2}, \frac{7}{2}, \frac{8}{2}, \frac{9}{2}, \frac{10}{2}$

b. $\frac{1}{3}, \frac{2}{3}, \frac{3}{3}, \frac{4}{3}, \frac{5}{3}, \frac{6}{3}, \frac{7}{3}, \frac{8}{3}, \frac{9}{3}$

c. $\frac{1}{4}, \frac{2}{4}, \frac{3}{4}, \frac{4}{4}, \frac{5}{4}, \frac{6}{4}, \frac{7}{4}, \frac{8}{4}, \frac{9}{4}, \frac{10}{4}, \frac{11}{4}, \frac{12}{4}$

2. List all the fractions that were located at a whole number in all three number lines that your group labeled.

3. What patterns do you see in all three labeled number lines?

_____

_____

iM KH

8.2: Locate 1 on the Number Line

1. Locate and label 1 on each number line. Be prepared to explain your reasoning.

a.

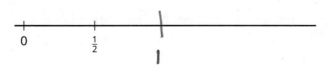

b.

c.

d.

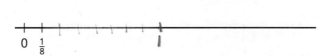

2. How could you locate 2 on the number lines in the previous problem?

by counting and making tick marks that mach the diomonator

Lesson 9: All Kinds of Numbers on the Number Line

- Let's locate numbers on the number line when we are given the location of one fraction.

Warm-up: Which One Doesn't Belong: Many Number Lines

Which one doesn't belong?

A

B

C

D

iM KH

9.1: Locate 1 Again

1. Locate and label 1 on each number line.

a.

b.

c.

2. Use any of the number lines to explain how you located 1.

_____

_____

9.2: Locate $\frac{3}{4}$

Locate and label $\frac{3}{4}$ on the number line. Be prepared to explain your reasoning.

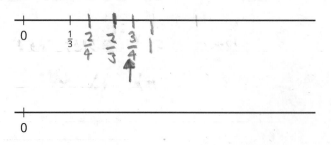

Section B Summary

In this section, we located and labeled fractions on the number line. We learned how to partition the number line from 0 to 1 to locate unit fractions.

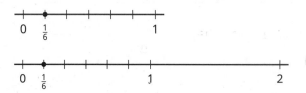

Then we used the location of unit fractions to locate other fractions.

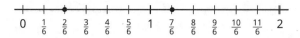

We also learned that some fractions are at the same location as whole numbers on the number line. Here, we can see that $\frac{6}{6}$ shares the same location as 1 and $\frac{12}{6}$ shares the same location as 2.

At the end of the section, we used our understanding of unit fractions to locate 1 on the number line when we only knew the location of a fraction.

Section B Practice Problems

1. a. Locate and label $\frac{1}{4}$ on the number line. Explain your reasoning.

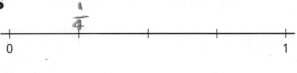

because there are four tick marks and that is one

b. Locate and label $\frac{1}{6}$ on the number line. Explain your reasoning.

because 6 tick marks that is one

(From Unit 5, Lesson 5.)

2. a. Locate and label $\frac{1}{8}$ on the number line.

b. Locate and label $\frac{1}{3}$ on the number line.

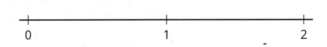

(From Unit 5, Lesson 6.)

3. a. Locate and label $\frac{4}{8}$ on the number line.

b. Locate and label $\frac{7}{6}$ on the number line.

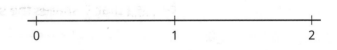

c. Diego marks and labels fourths on the number line like this:

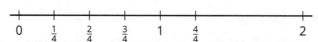

Do you agree with Diego? Explain your reasoning.

no because he labled $\frac{4}{4}$ after one but $\frac{4}{4} = 1$.

(From Unit 5, Lesson 7.)

4. a. Label the tick marks on the number line.

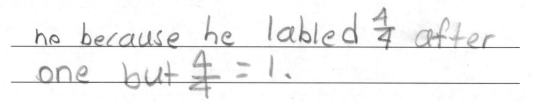

b. Which numbers on the number line are whole numbers? Explain how you know.

$1 = \frac{4}{4}$ because you Alredy had a whole split into 4 pieces and you have all the pieces $2 = double\ it$

(From Unit 5, Lesson 8.)

5. Locate and label 1 on the number line. Explain your reasoning.

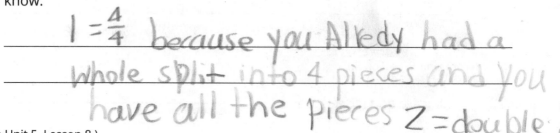

I labled it adding to what it shows

(From Unit 5, Lesson 9.)

6. Exploration

How are the fraction strip and number line the same? How are they different?

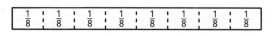

the fraction stips shows if you cut them in 8ths so it show ⅛ for every one the number line is counting up fractions or down.

7. Exploration

Han says that he can find 1 on the number line without finding $\frac{1}{8}$. What might Han's method be?

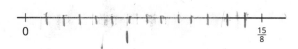

Han's method might be he would start a $\frac{15}{8}$ then count back by 8ths intill he gets to one.

Section C: Equivalent Fractions

Lesson 10: Equivalent Fractions

- Let's identify equivalent fractions.

iM KH

10.1: Equivalent to $\frac{1}{2}$

1. For which shapes is the shaded portion $\frac{1}{2}$ of the shape? Be prepared to share your reasoning.

A

B

C

D

E

F

2. How can there be more than one way of shading a shape to show $\frac{1}{2}$?

10.2: Find Equivalent Fractions

Use your fraction strips from an earlier lesson to find as many equivalent fractions as you can that are equivalent to:

1. $\frac{1}{2} = \frac{2}{4} = \frac{4}{8} = \frac{8}{16} = \frac{16}{32}$

2. $\frac{2}{3} = \frac{4}{6} = \frac{8}{12} = \frac{16}{24} = \frac{32}{48}$

3. $\frac{6}{6} = \frac{12}{12} = \frac{24}{24} = \frac{48}{48} = \frac{96}{96}$

4. $\frac{3}{4} = \frac{6}{8} = \frac{12}{16} = \frac{24}{32} = \frac{48}{64}$

Be prepared to show how you know the fractions are equivalent.

iM KH

Lesson 11: Generate Equivalent Fractions

- Let's generate equivalent fractions.

Warm-up: Number Talk: Something Times 8

Find the value of each expression mentally.

- 2×8

- 6×8

- 10×8

- 12×8

11.1: Show Equivalence

1. The diagram represents 1.

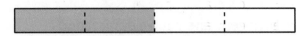

   a. What fraction does the shaded part of the diagram represent?

   $$\frac{2}{4}$$

   b. Jada says it represents $\frac{4}{8}$. Tyler is not so sure.

   Do you agree with Jada? If so, explain or show how you would convince Tyler that Jada is correct. If not, explain or show your reasoning.

   yes

2. Each diagram represents 1.

   a. Show that the shaded part of this diagram represents both $\frac{1}{3}$ and $\frac{2}{6}$.

   $\frac{2}{6}$
   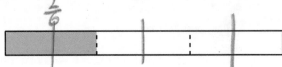

   b. Show that the shaded part represents both $\frac{6}{8}$ and $\frac{3}{4}$.

   $\frac{3}{4}$
   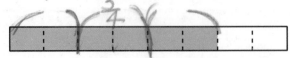

   c. Show that the shaded part represents both $\frac{6}{6}$ and $\frac{2}{2}$.

   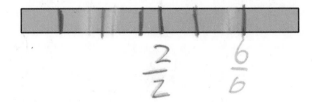

   $$\frac{2}{2} \qquad \frac{6}{6}$$

iM KH

11.2: More Than One Name

1. Each diagram represents 1. Write two fractions to represent the shaded part of each diagram.

   a. $\frac{4}{6}$ $\frac{2}{3}$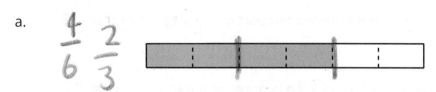

   b. $\frac{2}{8}$ $\frac{1}{4}$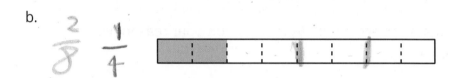

   c. $\frac{4}{4}$ $\frac{8}{8}$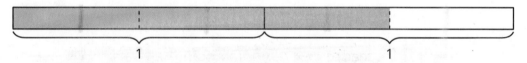

2. Here's another diagram.

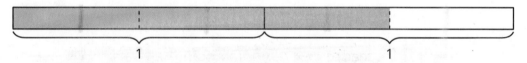

   a. What fraction does the shaded part of the diagram represent?

   $\frac{3}{2}$

   b. Write another fraction that it represents.

   $\frac{6}{4}$

Lesson 12: Equivalent Fractions on a Number Line

- Let's find fractions at the same location.

Warm-up: Notice and Wonder: Running on a Trail

What do you notice? What do you wonder?

Tyler ran part of the length of a trail.
Han ran part of the length of the same trail.

12.1: Running Part of a Trail

Some students are running on a trail at a park. Decide if each pair of students ran the same distance.

You can use number lines if they are helpful to you.

1. Elena ran $\frac{3}{6}$ of the trail.

   Han ran $\frac{1}{2}$ of the trail.

2. Jada ran $\frac{1}{4}$ of the trail.

   Kiran ran $\frac{2}{8}$ of the trail.

3. Lin ran $\frac{2}{3}$ of the trail.

   Mai ran $\frac{5}{6}$ of the trail.

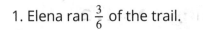

12.2: Locate and Pair

1. Locate and label the following numbers on a number line. You can use more than one number line if you wish.

$$\frac{1}{2}, \frac{1}{3}, \frac{1}{4}, \frac{2}{3}, \frac{2}{6}, \frac{3}{8}, \frac{3}{4}, \frac{4}{6}, \frac{4}{8}, \frac{6}{8}, \frac{7}{8}$$

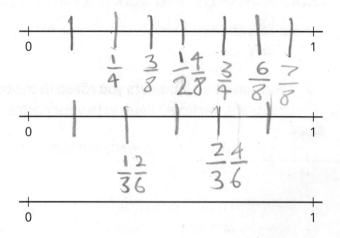

2. Find 4 pairs of fractions that are equivalent. Write equations to represent them.

$$\frac{1}{2} = \frac{2}{4} \qquad \frac{2}{3} = \frac{4}{6} \qquad \frac{1}{2} = \frac{4}{8} \qquad \frac{4}{8} = \frac{8}{16}$$

If you have time: Use the number lines to generate as many equivalent fractions as you can.

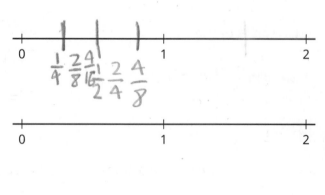

iM KH

12.3: Rolling for Equivalent Fractions

1. Roll 6 number cubes. If you roll any fives, they count as a wild card and can be any number you'd like.

2. Can you put the numbers you rolled in the boxes to make a statement that shows equivalent fractions? Work with your partner to find out.

3. If you cannot, re-roll as many number cubes as you'd like. You can re-roll your number cubes twice.

4. If you can make equivalent fractions, record your statement and show or explain how you know the fractions are equivalent. You get 1 point for each pair of equivalent fractions you write.

Round 1:

Show or explain how your fractions are equivalent.

Round 2:

Show or explain how your fractions are equivalent.

Round 3:

Show or explain how your fractions are equivalent.

Round 4:

Show or explain how your fractions are equivalent.

Round 5:

$$\frac{\square}{\square} = \frac{\square}{\square}$$

Show or explain how your fractions are equivalent.

Round 6:

$$\frac{\square}{\square} = \frac{\square}{\square}$$

Show or explain how your fractions are equivalent.

Round 7:

$$\frac{\square}{\square} = \frac{\square}{\square}$$

Show or explain how your fractions are equivalent.

Round 8:

$$\frac{\square}{\square} = \frac{\square}{\square}$$

Show or explain how your fractions are equivalent.

iM KH

Lesson 13: Whole Numbers and Fractions

- Let's find fractions and whole numbers that are equivalent.

Warm-up: Notice and Wonder: Four Number Lines

What do you notice? What do you wonder?

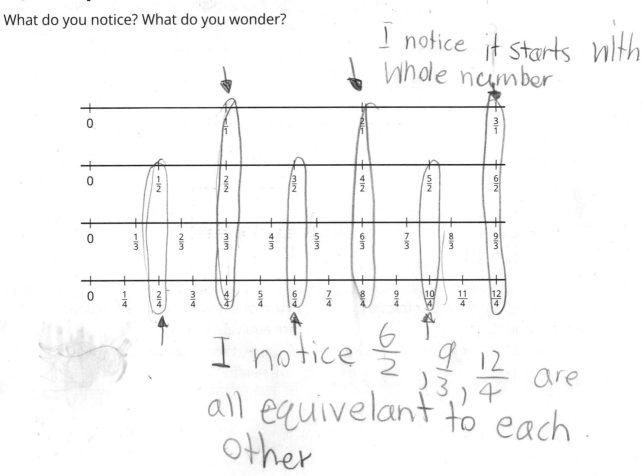

I notice it starts with whole number

I notice $\frac{6}{2}$, $\frac{9}{3}$, $\frac{12}{4}$ are all equivelant to each other

13.1: Hidden Whole Numbers

1. On each number line, circle the fractions that are equivalent to whole numbers. Explain how you know.

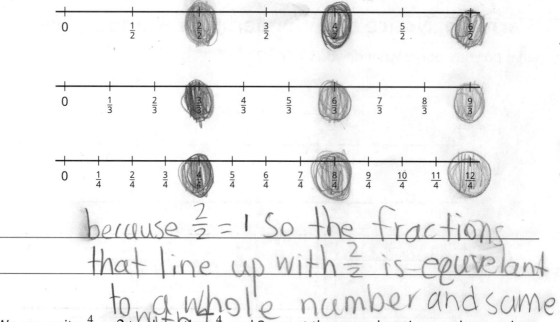

because $\frac{2}{2} = 1$ So the fractions that line up with $\frac{2}{2}$ is equivelant to a whole number and same

2. We can write $\frac{4}{2} = 2$ to show that $\frac{4}{2}$ and 2 are at the same location on the number line, so they are equivalent.

Write 5 other equations that show fractions that are equivalent to whole numbers. Use the number lines if they are helpful.

- $\frac{1}{4} + \frac{1}{4} + \frac{1}{4} + \frac{1}{4} = \frac{5}{4} \cdot \frac{5}{4} = 1$
- $\frac{1}{3} + \frac{1}{3} + \frac{1}{3} = \frac{3}{3} \quad \frac{3}{3} = 1$
- $\frac{1}{6} + \frac{1}{6} + \frac{1}{6} + \frac{1}{6} + \frac{1}{6} + \frac{1}{6} = \frac{6}{6} \quad \frac{6}{6} = 1$
- $\frac{1}{5} + \frac{1}{5} + \frac{1}{5} + \frac{1}{5} + \frac{1}{5} = \frac{5}{5} \quad \frac{5}{5} = 1$
- $\frac{1}{2} + \frac{1}{2} + \frac{1}{2} + \frac{1}{2} + \frac{1}{2} + \frac{1}{2} = \frac{6}{2} \quad \frac{6}{2} = 3$

$\frac{6}{2}$

iM KH

3. Decide if each fraction is equivalent to a whole number. Use number lines if they are helpful.

a. $\frac{11}{2}$

b. $\frac{5}{1}$

c. $\frac{12}{6}$

d. $\frac{10}{3}$

e. $\frac{12}{8}$

f. $\frac{16}{4}$

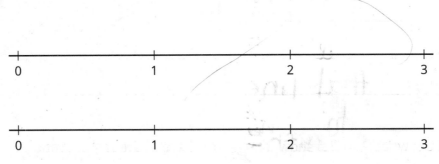

13.2: Write Them as Fractions

Work with your group to complete the table. In each column, write fractions that are equivalent to the whole number in the top row.

- Step 1: Write two fractions that are equivalent to each whole number (six fractions in all). Pass your paper to your right.

- Step 2: When you receive your neighbor's paper, write a new fraction that is equivalent to a whole number.

- Repeat Step 2 until the table is complete.

4	5	6
$\frac{4}{1}$	$\frac{5}{1}$	$\frac{6}{1}$
$\frac{8}{2}$	$\frac{10}{2}$	$\frac{12}{2}$
$\frac{32}{8}$	$\frac{20}{4}$	$\frac{18}{3}$
$\frac{16}{4}$	$\frac{40}{8}$	$\frac{24}{4}$
$\frac{64}{16}$	$\frac{30}{6}$	$\frac{36}{6}$
$\frac{8}{2}$	$\frac{60}{12}$	$\frac{48}{8}$

$$2 = \frac{4}{2}$$

iM KH

Section C Summary

In this section, we learned that different fractions can be equivalent. We know fractions are equivalent if they are the same size or located at the same location on the number line.

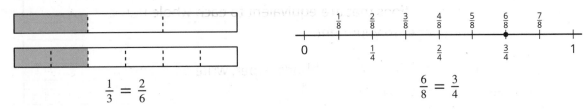

$$\frac{1}{3} = \frac{2}{6}$$

$$\frac{6}{8} = \frac{3}{4}$$

We also learned that some fractions are whole numbers, and that we can write whole numbers as fractions.

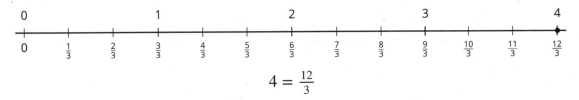

$$4 = \frac{12}{3}$$

Section C Practice Problems

1. Select **all** correct statements.

| $\frac{1}{2}$ | $\frac{1}{2}$ |

| $\frac{1}{3}$ | $\frac{1}{3}$ | $\frac{1}{3}$ |

| $\frac{1}{4}$ | $\frac{1}{4}$ | $\frac{1}{4}$ | $\frac{1}{4}$ |

| $\frac{1}{6}$ | $\frac{1}{6}$ | $\frac{1}{6}$ | $\frac{1}{6}$ | $\frac{1}{6}$ | $\frac{1}{6}$ |

A. $\frac{1}{2}$ is equivalent to $\frac{3}{6}$

B. $\frac{1}{2}$ is equivalent to $\frac{1}{3}$

C. $\frac{2}{2}$ is equivalent to $\frac{4}{4}$

D. $\frac{2}{2}$ is equivalent to $\frac{6}{6}$

E. $\frac{2}{3}$ is equivalent to $\frac{4}{6}$

F. $\frac{2}{3}$ is equivalent to $\frac{3}{4}$

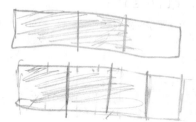

(From Unit 5, Lesson 10.)

2. Write as many fractions as you can that represent the shaded part of each diagram.

a

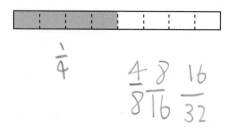

$$\frac{1}{4} \qquad \frac{4}{8} \quad \frac{8}{16} \quad \frac{16}{32}$$

b

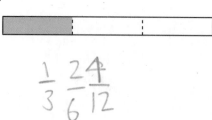

$$\frac{1}{3} \quad \frac{24}{6} \quad \frac{24}{12}$$

(From Unit 5, Lesson 11.)

iM KH

3. a. Tyler draws this picture and says that $\frac{3}{4}$ is equivalent to $\frac{2}{3}$. Explain why Tyler is not correct.

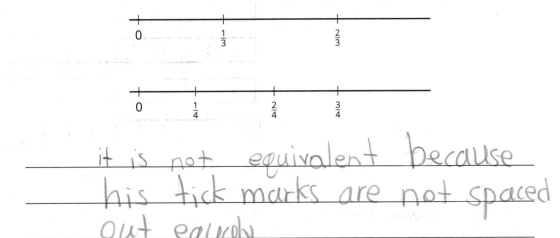

it is not equivalent because his tick marks are not spaced out equally

b. Find a fraction equivalent to $\frac{2}{3}$.

$\frac{4}{6}$

c. Find a fraction equivalent to $\frac{3}{4}$.

$\frac{6}{8}$

(From Unit 5, Lesson 12.)

4. a. Write 10 as a fraction in 2 different ways.

$\frac{20}{2}$ $\frac{40}{4}$

b. Is $\frac{88}{8}$ equivalent to a whole number?

no

(From Unit 5, Lesson 13.)

5. **Exploration**

Decide if each fraction is a whole number. Explain or show your reasoning.

a. $\frac{100}{2}$ yes $\frac{10}{2} = 5$ so $\frac{100}{2} = 50$ whole

b. $\frac{100}{3}$ no because you can never get $\frac{10}{3}$ on a whole number so you can't get $\frac{100}{3}$ on a whole number

c. $\frac{100}{4}$ no Because $\frac{100}{2}$ is on a whole number but $\frac{100}{4}$ is on not on a whole number because you cant get $\frac{10}{4}$ on a whole number

d. $\frac{100}{6}$ no Because you cant get 6 on a whole number cant get $\frac{10}{6}$ so you cant get $\frac{100}{6}$ on a whole number

e. $\frac{100}{8}$ no because you cant get $\frac{10}{8}$ on a whole number so you cant get $\frac{100}{8}$ on a whole number

6. **Exploration**

If you continue to fold fraction strips, how many parts can you fold them into? Can you fold them into 100 equal parts?

yes but it would take a long time

62

iM KH

Section D: Fraction Comparisons

Lesson 14: How Do You Compare Fractions?

- Let's represent and compare fractions.

Warm-up: Number Talk: Which Whole Numbers?

Find the whole number that each fraction is equivalent to.

- $\frac{16}{1}$

- $\frac{16}{2}$

- $\frac{16}{4}$

- $\frac{20}{4}$

14.1: Equivalent or Not?

Are these fractions equivalent? Show your thinking using diagrams, symbols, or other representations.

1. $\frac{1}{2}$ and $\frac{1}{3}$

2. $\frac{4}{6}$ and $\frac{5}{6}$

3. $\frac{3}{4}$ and $\frac{6}{8}$

14.2: Same Fractions, Different Result?

Han says $\frac{4}{6}$ is less than $\frac{5}{6}$. His work is shown.

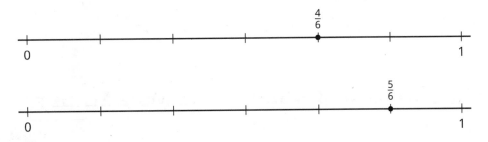

Lin says $\frac{4}{6}$ is greater than $\frac{5}{6}$. Her work is shown.

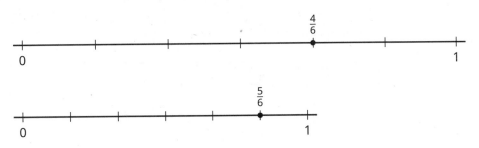

Why might Han and Lin make different comparison statements for the same fractions?

because Lin mad the four-6ths
number line biger than the five-sixths
so it apears bigger

Lesson 15: Compare Fractions with the Same Denominator

- Let's compare two fractions with the same denominator.

Warm-up: Notice and Wonder: Two More Strips

What do you notice? What do you wonder?

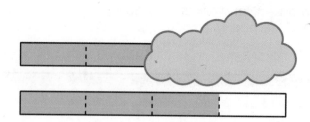

iM KH

15.1: Compare Fractions with the Same Denominator

1. For each pair of fractions, circle the fraction that is greater. Explain or show your reasoning.

   a. $\frac{1}{2}$ and $\boxed{\frac{3}{2}}$

   they are both using
   halfs and 3 is greater than 1

   b. $\boxed{\frac{3}{8}}$ and $\frac{2}{8}$

   they both using 8ths 3 is greater
   than 2

2. Use the symbols > or < to make each statement true. Explain or show your reasoning.

   a. $\frac{1}{6}$ ___<___ $\frac{4}{6}$

   1 is less than 4

   b. $\frac{4}{4}$ ___<___ $\frac{5}{4}$

   4 is less than 5

   c. $\frac{2}{3}$ ___>___ $\frac{1}{3}$

   2 is greater than 1

   d. $\frac{4}{8}$ ___<___ $\frac{6}{8}$

   4 is less than 6

If you have time: Write in the missing numerator of the fraction to make each statement true. Explain or show your reasoning.

1. $\frac{1}{2} < \frac{3}{2}$

3 is greater than 1

2. $\frac{6}{4} > \frac{3}{4}$

3 is Less than 6

3. $\frac{4}{3} < \frac{5}{3}$

5 is greater than 4

4. $\frac{5}{8} > \frac{3}{8}$

3 is Less than 5

5. $\frac{6}{7} > \frac{3}{7}$

6 is greater than 3

15.2: Spin to Win: Same Denominator

In this game, you will record fractions on number lines. Choose a writing utensil in a color different than your partner's so you can tell which fraction is whose on each number line.

1. Each player spins the paper clip. The player who spins the highest number is Player 1.

2. Player 1 chooses a denominator for the first round: 2, 3, 4, 6, or 8.

3. Each player spins for the numerator of their fraction.

4. Each player locates and labels their fraction on the same number line on the recording sheet.

5. The player with the greater fraction wins and picks the denominator for the next round.

6. Repeat for 10 rounds. The player who wins the most rounds wins the game.

Lesson 16: Compare Fractions with the Same Numerator

- Let's compare two fractions with the same numerator.

Warm-up: True or False: Unit Fractions

Decide whether each statement is true or false. Be prepared to explain your reasoning.

- $\frac{1}{2} > \frac{1}{4}$

- $\frac{1}{4} > \frac{1}{3}$

- $\frac{1}{6} > \frac{1}{8}$

iM KH

16.1: Five Parts of Something

1. Priya says that $\frac{5}{6}$ is greater than $\frac{5}{8}$.

    Tyler says that $\frac{5}{8}$ is greater than $\frac{5}{6}$.

    Who do you agree with? Show your thinking using diagrams or number lines.

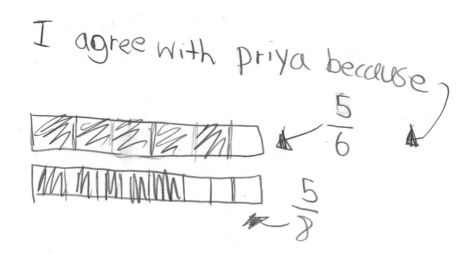

I agree with priya because

$\frac{5}{6}$

$\frac{5}{8}$

2. For each pair of fractions, which fraction do you think is greater?

    a. $\frac{5}{3}$ or $\frac{5}{4}$ $\frac{5}{3}$

    b. $\frac{5}{8}$ or $\frac{5}{2}$ $\frac{5}{2}$

    c. $\frac{5}{6}$ or $\frac{5}{4}$ $\frac{5}{4}$

3. Locate and label each fraction on a number line: $\frac{5}{2}, \frac{5}{3}, \frac{5}{4}, \frac{5}{6}, \frac{5}{8}$.

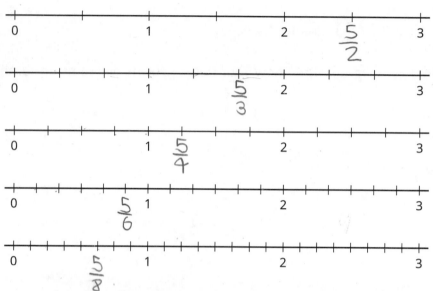

What do you notice about the points? Make 1–2 observations.

each time the pices get smaller
it got farther away from big
whole numbers and closer to
one and then even got closer
to zero

16.2: Fractions with the Same Numerator

1. For each pair of fractions, circle the fraction that is greater. Explain or show your reasoning.

   a. $\frac{1}{4}$ and $\frac{1}{3}$

   b. $\frac{3}{4}$ and $\frac{3}{8}$

   c. $\frac{5}{3}$ and $\frac{5}{6}$

   d. $\frac{9}{8}$ and $\frac{9}{6}$

2. Use the symbols > or < to make each statement true. Be prepared to explain your reasoning.

   a. $\frac{2}{2}$ $>$ $\frac{2}{6}$ $\frac{2}{2} = 1$ $\frac{2}{6} \neq 1$

   b. $\frac{4}{3}$ $>$ $\frac{4}{8}$ $\frac{4}{3} = $ more than

   c. $\frac{8}{8}$ _____ $\frac{8}{4}$

d. $\frac{5}{4}$ _____ $\frac{5}{3}$

3. Write in the missing denominator of the fraction to make each statement true. Be prepared to explain your reasoning.

   a. $\frac{1}{3} < \frac{1}{\rule{2em}{0.4pt}}$

   b. $\frac{6}{4} > \frac{6}{\rule{2em}{0.4pt}}$

   c. $\frac{4}{4} < \frac{4}{\rule{2em}{0.4pt}}$

   d. $\frac{2}{6} < \frac{2}{\rule{2em}{0.4pt}}$

Lesson 17: Compare Fractions

- Let's compare more fractions in different situations.

Warm-up: Estimation Exploration: Ladybug Length

What is the length of this ladybug?

Record an estimate that is:

too low	about right	too high

17.1: Comparison Problems

For each problem:

- Answer the question and explain or show your reasoning.
- Represent your answer with a statement that uses the symbols >, <, or =.

1. A beetle crawled $\frac{2}{8}$ of the length of a log. A caterpillar crawled $\frac{2}{3}$ of the length of the same log. Which insect crawled farther?

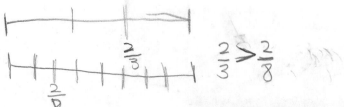

$$\frac{2}{3} > \frac{2}{8}$$

2. A grasshopper is 4 centimeters long. A caterpillar is $\frac{12}{3}$ centimeters long. Which insect is longer?

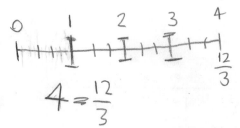

$$4 = \frac{12}{3}$$

4 centimeters

3. A ladybug crawled $\frac{3}{8}$ the length of a branch. An ant crawled $\frac{5}{8}$ the length of the same branch. Which insect crawled farther?

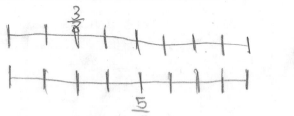

$$\frac{3}{8} < \frac{5}{8}$$

4. A grasshopper jumped $\frac{5}{8}$ the width of the sidewalk. A frog jumped $\frac{5}{6}$ the width of the same sidewalk. Which jumped a longer distance?

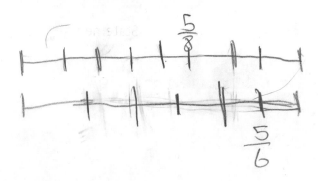

iM KH

17.2: What Fraction Makes Sense?

1. Oh, no! Some juice spilled on Noah's fractions. Help him figure out what was written before the juice was spilled.

   Find as many numbers as you can to make each statement true. Explain or show your reasoning.

   a.

   $$\frac{2}{8} < \frac{*}{8} \qquad \frac{2}{8} < \frac{3}{8}$$

   b.

   $$\frac{3}{6} = * \qquad \frac{3}{6} = \frac{1}{2}$$

   c.

   $$\frac{4}{3} > \frac{4}{*} \qquad \frac{4}{3} > \frac{4}{8}$$

2. For each fraction, find a fraction that is less, one that is greater, and one that is equivalent. Then, write a statement that uses the symbols >, <, or = to record each comparison.

   a. Less than $\frac{4}{6}$: _____   Statement: $\frac{3}{6}$

   More than $\frac{4}{6}$: _____   Statement: $\frac{5}{6}$

   Equivalent to $\frac{4}{6}$: _____   Statement: $\frac{8}{12}$

   b. Less than $\frac{3}{4}$: _____   Statement: $\frac{2}{4}$

   More than $\frac{3}{4}$: _____   Statement: $\frac{4}{4}$

   Equivalent to $\frac{3}{4}$: _____   Statement: $\frac{6}{8}$

17.3: Ultimate Locate and Label

Locate and label each fraction on the number line. Be prepared to share your reasoning.

$$\frac{1}{2}, \frac{3}{8}, \frac{13}{8}, \frac{2}{4}, \frac{3}{4}, \frac{9}{8}, \frac{5}{4}, \frac{12}{6}, \frac{5}{2}, \frac{9}{3}, \frac{20}{8}$$

```
+-----------------+-----------------+-----------------+
0                 1                 2                 3
```

Section D Summary

In this section, we compared fractions with the same numerator or denominator and used the symbols >, =, or < to record our results. We used diagrams and number lines to represent our thinking.

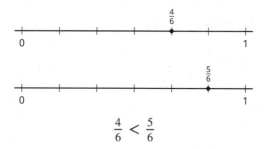

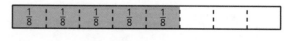

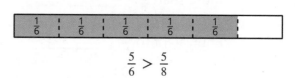

$$\frac{4}{6} < \frac{5}{6}$$

$$\frac{5}{6} > \frac{5}{8}$$

iM KH

Lesson 18: Design With Fractions

- Let's use fractions to create a design.

Warm-up: Notice and Wonder: Between 0 and 1

What do you notice? What do you wonder?

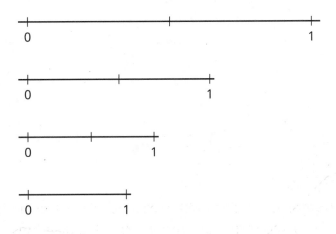

18.1: Design With $\frac{1}{2}$

1. Here is a square. On each side, mark a point to show $\frac{1}{2}$ of its length.

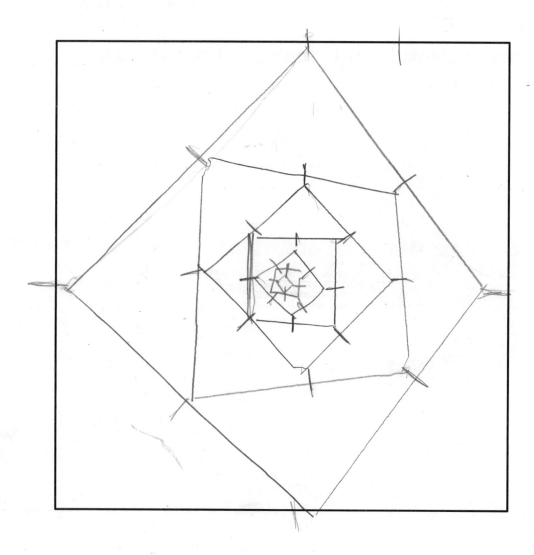

Connect each point to the point on the two sides next to it. What shape did you create?

2. Look at the new shape you created. On each side, mark a point to show $\frac{1}{2}$ of its length. Connect the points again. What shape did you create?

3. Repeat the steps you just did at least two more times. Make some observations about the design you just created.

18.2: Design With $\frac{1}{4}$

1. Here is another square. On each side, mark a point to show $\frac{1}{4}$ of its length.

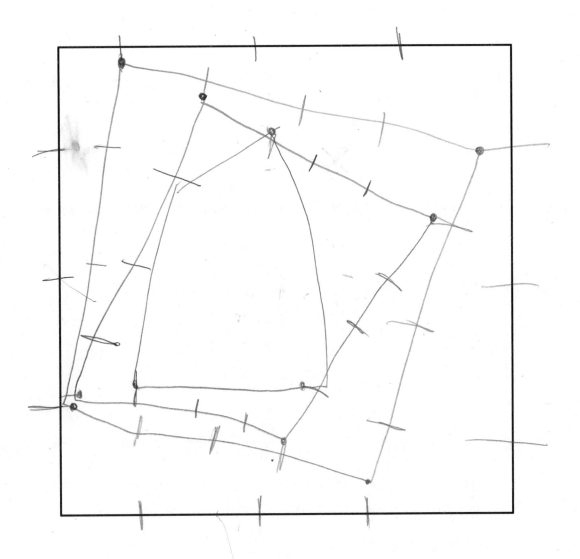

Connect each point to the point on the two sides next to it. What shape did you create?

2. Look at the new shape you created. On each side, mark a point to show $\frac{1}{4}$ of its length. Connect the points again. What shape did you create?

3. Repeat the steps you just did at least two more times. Make some observations about the design you just created.

Section D Practice Problems

1. a. Are $\frac{2}{3}$ and $\frac{4}{6}$ equivalent? Show your thinking using diagrams, symbols, or other representations.

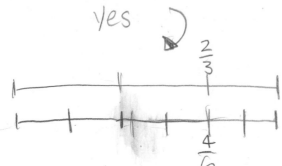

b. Are $\frac{6}{8}$ and $\frac{7}{8}$ equivalent? Show your thinking using diagrams, symbols, or other representations.

(From Unit 5, Lesson 14.)

2. Han says there is no fraction with denominator 8 that's greater than $\frac{8}{8}$ because $\frac{8}{8}$ is a whole. Do you agree with Han? Explain your reasoning.

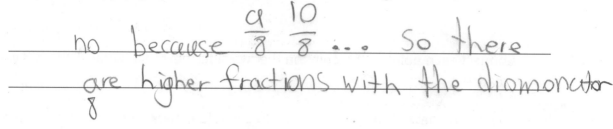

no because $\frac{9}{8}$ $\frac{10}{8}$ ... So there are higher fractions with the diomonctor $\frac{}{8}$

(From Unit 5, Lesson 15.)

iM KH

3. Use the symbols > or < to make each statement true. Explain your reasoning.

a. $\frac{5}{3}$ ___ $\frac{5}{2}$

You can have ↘

b. $\frac{3}{4}$ ___ < ___ $\frac{5}{4}$

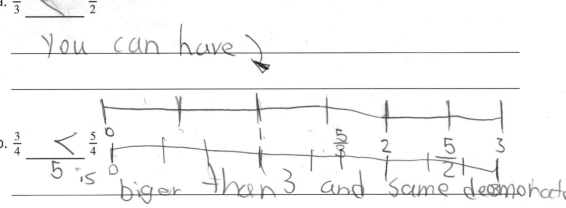

5 is biger than 3 and same desmohador

(From Unit 5, Lesson 16.)

4. a. Jada threw the ball $\frac{3}{4}$ of the length of the gym. Clare threw the ball $\frac{6}{8}$ of the length of the gym. Clare says she threw the ball farther. Do you agree? Show your thinking.

no $\frac{3}{4} = \frac{6}{8}$ $\frac{3 \times 2 = 6}{4 \times 2 = 8}$ ✓

b. Tyler kicked the ball $\frac{7}{8}$ the length of the playground. Andre kicked the ball $\frac{7}{6}$ the length of the playground. Andre says he kicked the ball farther. Do you agree? Show your thinking.

Yes $\frac{7}{8}$ = Less than 1
       $\frac{7}{6}$ = more than 1

(From Unit 5, Lesson 17.)

5. **Exploration**

Clare walked $\frac{3}{4}$ of the way around a park. Tyler walked $\frac{3}{6}$ of the way around a different park. Who walked farther? Explain your reasoning.

6. **Exploration**

Choose a fraction that you can compare with both $\frac{3}{8}$ and $\frac{5}{6}$ by looking at the numerators and denominators.

iM KH

GRADE 3
Unit

6

Section A: Measurement Data on Line Plots

Lesson 1: Measure in Halves of an Inch

- Let's measure the length of objects around the room.

Warm-up: What Do You Know About Inches?

What do you know about inches?

an inch is about 2 cetimeters

you can measeare (type of measerment)s using inches

abriviation is "in"

12 in = foot

a e D d d

1.1: Measure Around the Room

Use the ruler from your teacher to measure the length of objects in the room. Be prepared to discuss your reasoning.

object	length (inches)
green duck	1 in
Arjun's water	8 in
pencil sharpener	2 in
Aadyah's head	8 in
Mr. chewy nat	9 in
eraser	5 in
My foot	9 in

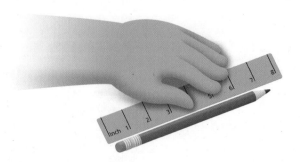

iM KH

1.2: Partition Inches into Halves

You will need one ruler from an earlier activity.

1. Work with your partner to partition every inch on the ruler into halves of an inch.

2. Use the ruler marked with halves of an inch to measure some lengths around the room.

object	length (inches)
desk	$32\frac{1}{2}$
Word study pouch	5 in
Pencil	7 in

because the numbers are like whole numbers and you can mark fractions on it

Lesson 2: Measure in Fourths of an Inch

- Let's measure lengths in quarters of an inch.

Warm-up: Estimation Exploration: Measure in Inches

What is the length of the paper clip?

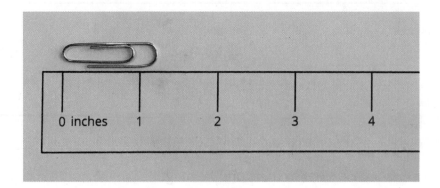

Record an estimate that is:

too low	just right	too high
$\frac{1}{2}$ in	1 in	2 in

iM KH

2.1: Partition Inches into Fourths

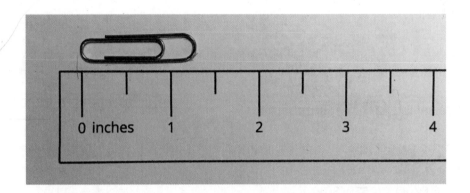

You will need the ruler that was not partitioned in an earlier activity.

1. With your partner, partition the ruler to show fourths of an inch.

2. Take turns using this ruler to measure the length of 4 objects around the room.

object	length
glue stick	4 in
green duck pencil top	$1\frac{1}{4}$ in
Siccors	$5\frac{1}{4}$
Sharpi	$5\frac{2}{4}$

2.2: Find Some Lengths

You will need the rulers you partitioned for this activity.

With your partner:

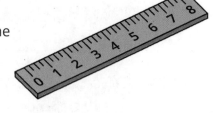

- Find at least 4 objects in the classroom that have the lengths shown in the table.

- Practice saying each measurement.

- Record the object in the table. If you find an object that is a whole number plus a fraction of an inch, write the exact measurement.

object	length
Sicky note	$2\frac{1}{2}$ inches
rain toper	$1\frac{1}{4}$ inches
Small blue pencil	$3\frac{3}{4}$ inches
math page	$8\frac{1}{2}$ inches
paper clip	a whole number of inches
Mr chewy nut's tail	a whole number and $\frac{1}{4}$ inches
	a whole number and $\frac{2}{4}$ inches
	a whole number and $\frac{3}{4}$ inches

iM KH

Lesson 3: Measure in Halves and Fourths of an Inch

- Let's measure lengths in halves of an inch and quarters of an inch.

Warm-up: Notice and Wonder: Rulers

Look at the rulers you have been using to measure and the ruler your teacher gave you.

What do you notice? What do you wonder?

3.1: Halves and Quarters

1. Kiran and Jada are discussing the length of a worm.

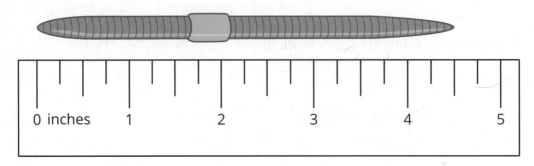

- Kiran says that the worm is $4\frac{2}{4}$ inches long.
- Jada says that the worm is $4\frac{1}{2}$ inches long.

Use the ruler to explain how both of their measurements are correct.

they both are correct because $\frac{2}{4}$ is equivelant to $\frac{1}{2}$ so they are both correct

2. Measure the length of the following worms.

A

$4\frac{1}{4}$ in

B

6 in

C

$2\frac{1}{4}$

D

$3\frac{1}{2}$

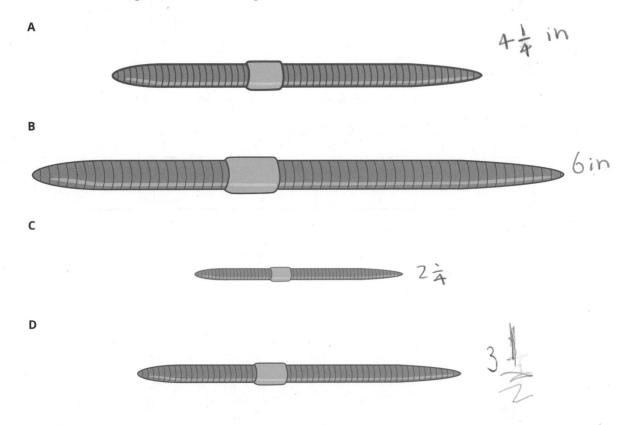

iM KH

3.2: Measure and Describe

1. Use the ruler you received today to measure some objects around the room.

   Find at least 1 object whose length is a whole number of inches and at least 3 objects whose lengths are not whole numbers.

object	length

2. Trade lists with another group. Find a length that could be written a different way.

object	length	equivalent length

Lesson 4: Interpret Measurement Data on Line Plots

- Let's make sense of line plots with lengths in half inches and quarter inches.

Warm-up: Notice and Wonder: A List and a Line Plot

What do you notice? What do you wonder?

Lengths in Inches

3	5	4	4	5	6	7	5
3	4	4	5	6	6	4	

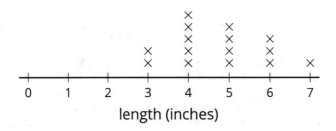

it is based of of
the chart

iM KH

4.1: A Set of Seedlings

heights of seedlings (in inches)

$\frac{1}{2}$	1	1	$\frac{1}{2}$	$1\frac{1}{2}$	$2\frac{1}{2}$	4	$\frac{1}{2}$
3	$1\frac{1}{2}$	5	$1\frac{1}{2}$	$1\frac{1}{2}$	$2\frac{1}{2}$	3	$\frac{1}{2}$
$2\frac{1}{2}$	$1\frac{1}{2}$	1	$1\frac{1}{2}$	4	2		

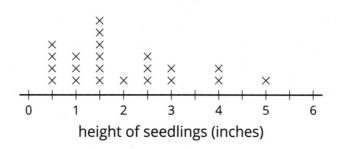

height of seedlings (inches)

1. Write 3 statements about the measurements represented in the line plot.

    it is based off of the chart
    the most cheeked of nuber is $\frac{1}{2}$
    they dident lable the halfs

2. What questions could be answered more easily with the line plot than the list?
   Write at least 2 questions.

    how many all together
    how much more $\frac{1}{2}$ than 5
    how much more 1 than 4

4.2: All About Twigs

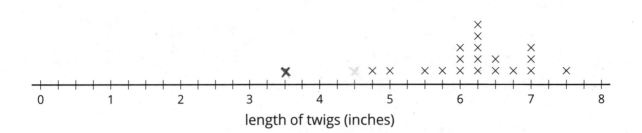

length of twigs (inches)

1. How many twig lengths are represented in the line plot?

    19

2. How many of the twigs are $6\frac{1}{2}$ inches long?

    2

3. How many of the twigs are less than 6 inches long?

    3

4. How many of the twigs are more than 6 inches long?

    12

5. What is the length of the shortest twig?

    $4\frac{3}{4}$

6. What is the length of the longest twig?

    $7\frac{2}{4}$

7. What is the most common twig length?

    $6\frac{1}{4}$

8. Add an "x" to the line plot that would represent a twig with a length between 3 and 4 inches.

    What is the length of the twig you added to the line plot?

    $3\frac{1}{2}$

iM KH

Lesson 5: Represent Measurement Data on Line Plots

- Let's collect measurement data and show them on a line plot.

Warm-up: Number Talk: Multiply Teen Numbers

Find the value of each expression mentally.

- 3×10 =30

- 3×13 =39

- 6×13 78

- 3×26 78

5.1: Go for a Measurement Walk

1. What objects will you measure?

2. Record the lengths of the objects in the table (or on another sheet of paper).

object	length (inches)	object	length (inches)
Water botle	7 $\frac{3}{4}$ in		
banana	7 in		
hair	9 in		
mini whiteboard eraser	4 $\frac{1}{2}$ in		
Dana's head	8 $\frac{1}{2}$		
ear	2 in		
my ear	1 $\frac{1}{2}$		
lenth of sentence	9 in		
word republic	4 $\frac{1}{2}$		
my name	2 in		
hair (gabrial)	4 $\frac{1}{2}$		

5.2: Let's Make a Line Plot

Create a line plot to represent the measurement data you collected. You will display and share your line plot with your class later.

You can use the blank number line here for your draft. Think about:

- how to label the tick marks so that all the measurements are included

- details to help others understand the data you collected

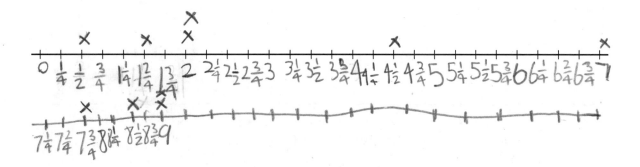

Section A Summary

In this section, we learned how to measure lengths using rulers marked with halves and quarters of an inch.

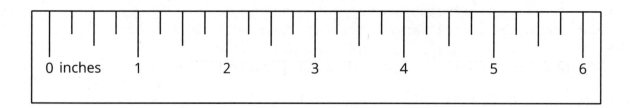

We also learned to make line plots to show measurements in half inches or quarter inches.

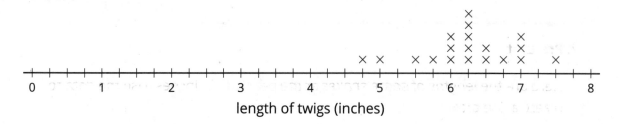

length of twigs (inches)

iM KH

Section A Practice Problems

1. Pre-unit

What is the length of the pencil in centimeters? Show your reasoning.

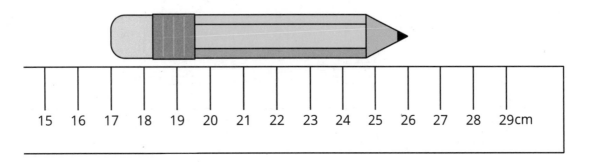

2. Pre-unit

Here are the lengths of some snakes at the pet store in inches. Use the data to create a line plot.

8	10	13	13	13
15	15	18	21	22

3. Pre-unit

Find the value of each sum or difference.

    a. $374 + 455$

    b. $259 - 186$

4. Pre-unit

Write the time shown on each clock.

a

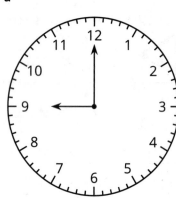

b

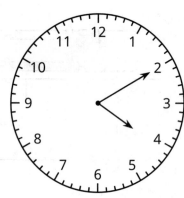

c

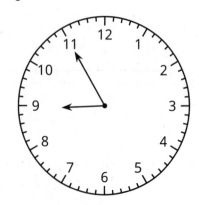

a. _____

b. _____

c. _____

iM KH

5. **Pre-unit**

Find the value of each expression.

a. $8 \times 9 = 72$

b. $16 \times 6 = 96$

c. $72 \div 8 = 9$

d. $92 \div 4 = 23$

6. Find the length of each pencil.

a.

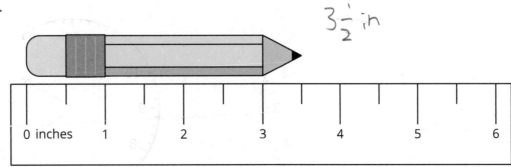

$3\frac{1}{2}$ in

b.

4 in

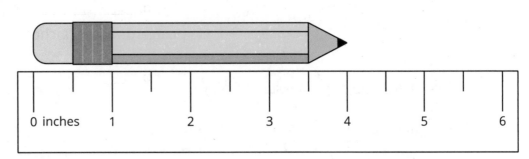

(From Unit 6, Lesson 1.)

7. a. Partition the ruler into halves of an inch and then quarters of an inch.

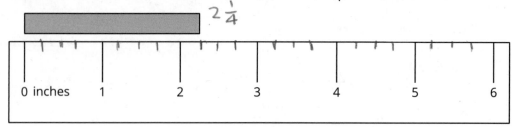

$2\frac{1}{4}$

    b. What is the length of the rectangle? Explain or show your reasoning.

(From Unit 6, Lesson 2.)

8. Here are the lengths of some pieces of pasta in inches.

Which lengths are the same? Explain or show your reasoning.

$3\frac{2}{4}$ 2 $3\frac{1}{2}$ $\frac{4}{2}$

they are not the same because they are all difrent numbers

(From Unit 6, Lesson 3.)

9. The line plot shows the width of some postcards in inches.

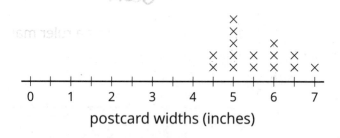

postcard widths (inches)

   a. How many postcards measured $5\frac{1}{2}$ inches?

2

   b. How many postcards measured 6 inches or more?

6

   c. How many postcards were measured for the line plot?

(From Unit 6, Lesson 4.)

15

iM KH

10. Here are the lengths of some straws in inches. Represent the data on a line plot.

$$4\frac{3}{4} \qquad 5\frac{1}{2} \qquad 4\frac{1}{4} \qquad 5\frac{2}{4} \qquad 4\frac{1}{2} \qquad 3\frac{3}{4}$$

$$5\frac{1}{4} \qquad 4\frac{2}{4} \qquad 5 \qquad 4\frac{1}{4} \qquad 4\frac{1}{2}$$

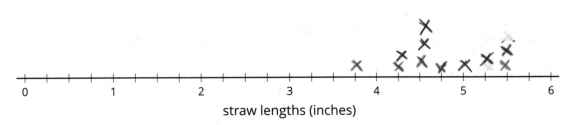

straw lengths (inches)

(From Unit 6, Lesson 5.)

11. **Exploration**

You will need a ruler marked in $\frac{1}{4}$ inches for this problem.

a. For each length, pick an object in the classroom or at home that you think will be close to that length.

■ $1\frac{1}{2}$ inches   Dencil toper

■ 7 inches   pencil

■ 33 inches   desk

b. Measure each object using a ruler marked in $\frac{1}{4}$ inches. Was each estimate too high, too low, or just right?

12. **Exploration**

Choose a collection of objects to measure at school or at home. Make a line plot of the length of the objects.

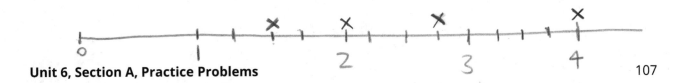

Section B: Weight and Liquid Volume
Lesson 6: Estimate and Measure Weight

- Let's measure and estimate weight.

Warm-up: Notice and Wonder: Produce Stand

What do you notice? What do you wonder?

wonder- how much did this cost

iM KH

6.1: Estimate Weight

This paper clip weighs *about* 1 gram.   This basket of apples weighs *about* 1 kilogram.

1. For each weight measurement, find an example of something you think has about the same weight.

   a. 1 gram   Paper clips

   b. 10 grams   pencil

   c. 100 grams   Waterbotle

   d. 1 kilogram   basket apples

   e. 2 kilograms   plasic chair

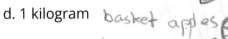

2. Find some objects in the room that belong in each column based on their weight.

less than 1 gram	between 1 gram and 100 grams	between 100 grams and 1 kilogram	more than 1 kilogram
braclet	Apple	Ipod	chair
lead	Pencil	Water botte (empty)	table
squishi	catty	Workbook	door
paperclip	earasor	back pack	desk

6.2: The Weight of Pets

Match each pet to the amount that could be its weight. Explain your reasoning.

pet   weight

1. guinea pig

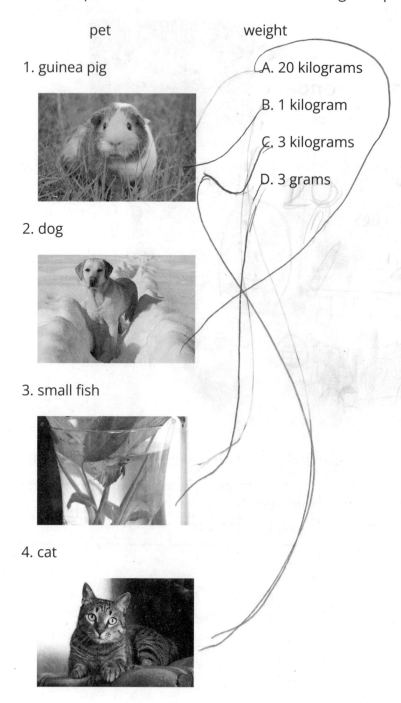

                                 A. 20 kilograms

                                 B. 1 kilogram

                                 C. 3 kilograms

                                 D. 3 grams

2. dog

3. small fish

4. cat

Lesson 7: Introduction to Liquid Volume

- Let's learn about liquid volume.

Warm-up: Notice and Wonder: The Bowl and the Jar

What do you notice? What do you wonder?

there is water in both
of them

I'm hungrey
pov

7.1: Liquid Volume Estimation Exploration

Your teacher will give you two containers labeled "A" and "B," and another container labeled "unit."

1. How many units do you think container A will hold?

    Record an estimate that is:

too low	about right	too high
2	15	40

2. How many units do you think container B will hold?

    Record an estimate that is:

too low	about right	too high
3	15	60

3. Use the unit container to compare the liquid volume that containers A and B hold. Which container holds the greater volume? How do you know?

    it is the same volume

iM KH

7.2: Liquid Volume in Liters

How many liters of water will fit in the large container?

Record an estimate that is:

too low	about right	too high
1	25	50

Lesson 8: Estimate and Measure Liquid Volume

- Let's measure and estimate liquid volume.

Warm-up: Number Talk: Divide by 3

Find the value of each expression mentally.

- $30 \div 3 = 10$

- $60 \div 3 = 20$

- $63 \div 3 = 21$

- $54 \div 3 = 18$

8.1: Estimate Liquid Volume

1. Clare says the bathtub holds about 2 liters.

   Jada says the bathtub holds about 20 liters.

   Kiran says the bathtub holds about 200 liters.

   Whom do you agree with? Explain or show your reasoning.

   I agree with Kiran because I don't think this tub will fit 200 liter

2. Would the bucket and the bottle hold 2 liters, 20 liters, or 200 liters? Explain how you know.

   I think 20 Liters because it looks medium

   It look likes a 2 liter bott

3. Match the containers to the number of liters they could hold. Be ready to explain your reasoning.

item

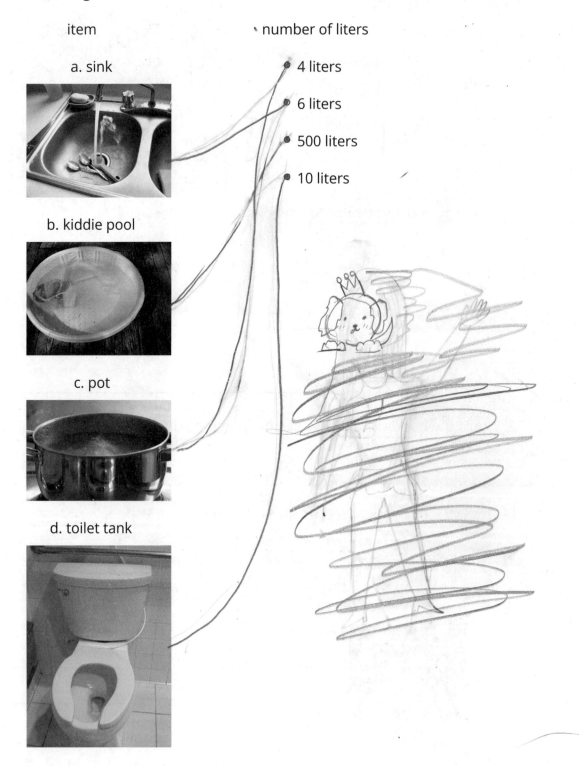

a. sink

b. kiddie pool

c. pot

d. toilet tank

number of liters

4 liters

6 liters

500 liters

10 liters

iM KH

8.2: Measure Liquid Volume

What do you notice? What do you wonder?

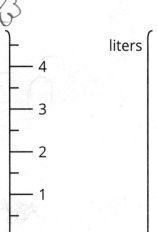

liters

4

3

2

1

0 inches   1   2   3   4   5   6

1. The container in each image is marked in liters. Find the volume of the liquid.

A

3L

B

5L

C

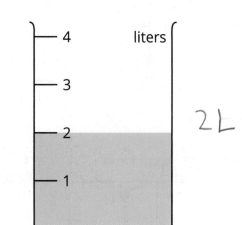

2L

D

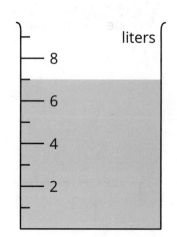

6½ L

E

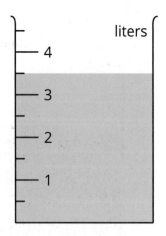

$3\frac{1}{2}$ L

F

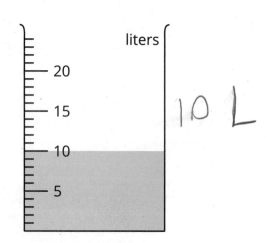

10 L

iM KH

G

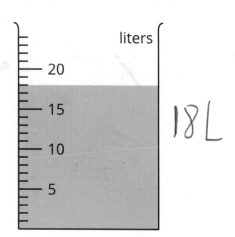

18L

H

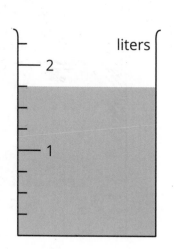

1 $\frac{3}{4}$

2. Shade the images of the empty containers to show the liquid volume.

P: 1 liter

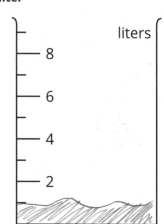

Q: 8 liters

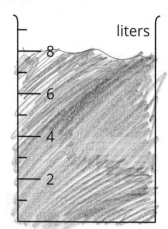

R: 7 liters

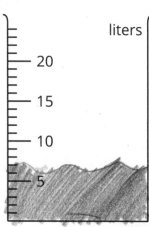

S: $2\frac{1}{2}$ **liters**

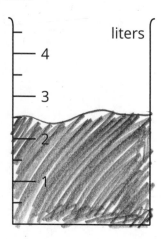

T: 23 liters

liters

20

15

10

5

3. If you have time: Of all the containers in this activity, which two containers have the most liquid? How many liters would you have if you combined the liquid in them? Explain or show your reasoning.

T And Q

23 +18 = 41

Section B Summary

In this section, we learned how to measure and estimate weight in grams and kilograms.

This paper clip weighs *about* 1 gram.   This basket of apples weighs *about* 1 kilogram.

We also learned how to measure and estimate liquid volume in liters.

Section B Practice Problems

1.   a. Circle the items that might weigh about 1 gram.

   a piece of   a turtle   a dollar bill   a chair   a pen
   gum

   b. Circle the items that might weigh about 1 kilogram.

   a giant   a pencil   a pineapple   a large book   a full
   tortoise   lunchbox

(From Unit 6, Lesson 6.)

2. For each item, decide whether it holds more than a liter, less than a liter, or about a liter.

   a. a bathtub   _____

   b. a cup   _____

   c. a swimming pool   _____

   d. a small pot for a plant   _____

(From Unit 6, Lesson 7.)

3.   a. What is the volume of liquid shown in the container?

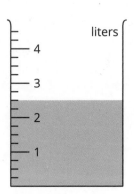

iM KH

b. Shade the image of the empty container to show $1\frac{3}{4}$ liters of water.

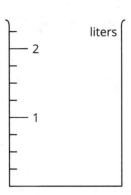

(From Unit 6, Lesson 8.)

4. **Exploration**

Kiran thinks that weight and volume go together. The bigger something is, the heavier it is and the heavier something is the bigger it is. Do you agree with Kiran? Give some examples to explain your thinking.

_____

_____

_____

_____

5. **Exploration**

You have a 3 liter jug of water and a 5 liter jug of water. How can you measure out 4 liters of water precisely using these two jugs?

Section C: Problems Involving Time

Lesson 9: Time to the Nearest Minute

- Let's tell and write time to the nearest minute.

Warm-up: Estimation Exploration: On the One Hand . . . .

This clock only has an hour hand.

What time could it be?

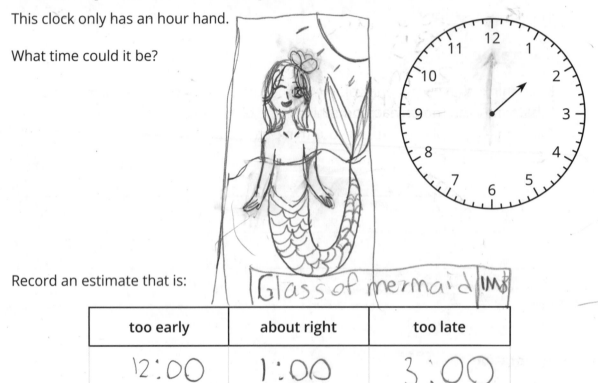

Record an estimate that is:

too early	about right	too late
12:00	1:00	3:00

9.1: Just a Clock on the Wall

1. Lin says the time shown on the clock is 1:37 p.m.

   Diego says the time is 1:35 p.m.

   Who do you agree with? Explain or show your reasoning.

Lin because
is ___:30 and
is ___:35
and 2 more is
___:37 and it's 1:37

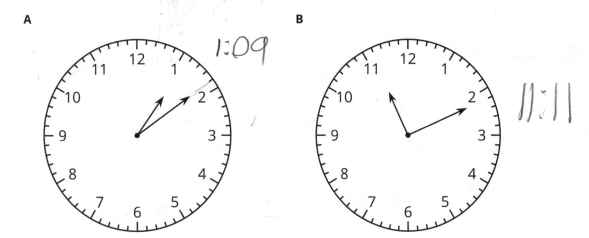

2. What time is shown on each clock?

A

1:09

B

11:11

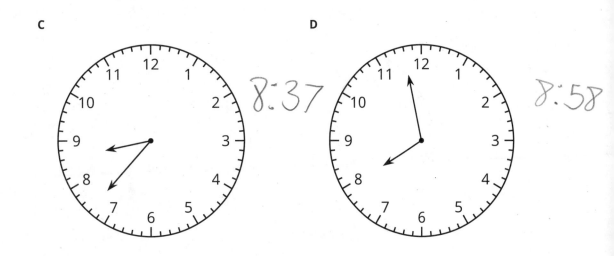

C

8:37

D

8:58

9.2: Show Time

1. Show the time given on each clock.

A 2:36 PM

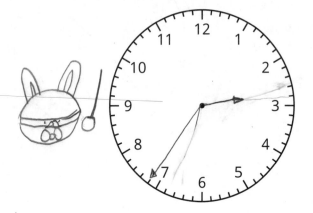

B 3:18 PM

C 12:17 PM

D 9:02 PM

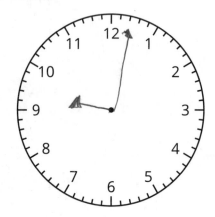

2. Draw a time on this clock. Trade with a partner and tell the time on their clock.

iM KH

Lesson 10: Solve Problems Involving Time (Part 1)

- Let's solve problems involving time.

10.1: Time at the Bus Stop

1. Kiran arrived at the bus stop at 3:27 p.m., as shown on this clock. He waited 24 minutes for his bus to arrive.

   What time did his bus arrive? Show your thinking. Organize it so it can be followed by others.

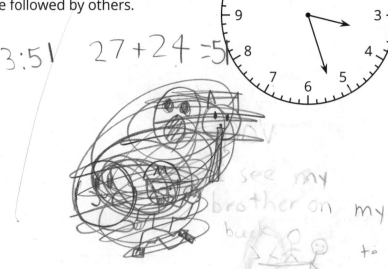

3:51   27 + 24 = 5

see my brother on my back to

2. Elena arrived at the bus stop at 3:45 p.m. She also waited 24 minutes for her bus to arrive.

   What time did the bus arrive? Show your thinking. Organize it so it can be followed by others.

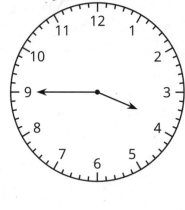

4:09

45 + 24 = 69

60 = hour

iM KH

10.2: Time on the Bus

Here's another problem about time:

At 6:32 p.m., Elena got on a bus to go home. She got off the bus at 7:10 p.m. How long was her bus ride?

Which strategy or representation would you use when solving a problem like this? Explain your reasoning.

her bus ride was 38 mins
Long because

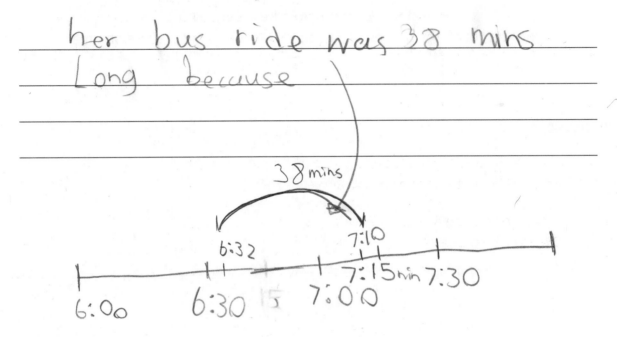

Lesson 11: Solve Problems Involving Time (Part 2)

- Let's solve more problems involving time.

Warm-up: Notice and Wonder: Band Practice

What do you notice? What do you wonder?

Han ate his dinner before he caught a bus.
When he got off the bus, he had to hurry to get to band practice on time.

iM KH

11.1: On the Bus Again

1. For how many minutes was Han on the bus? Explain or show your reasoning.

the time Han got on the bus: the time Han got off the bus:

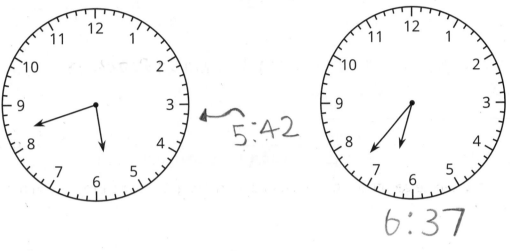

5:42

6:37

55 mins   55 mins

42 + 37 = 5:42 mins

55 mins = 6:37

2. Draw the minute hand to show that Elena waited for the bus for 32 minutes.

the time Elena started waiting: the time Elena got on the bus:

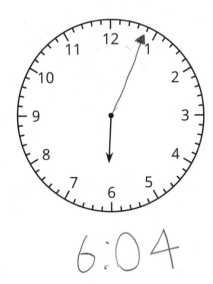

6:04

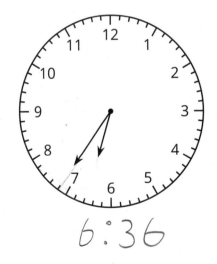

6:36

11.2: Math Libs Time

For each problem, fill in a name and an activity, and then solve the problem. Show your thinking. Organize it so it can be followed by others.

1. ___Lina___ started ___trick or treating___ at 8:25 a.m. and finished at 8:50 a.m. How much time was spent doing that activity?

    25 mins because 25+25=50

2. ___Andre___ finished ___eating___ at 5:38 p.m, after spending 20 minutes. What was the start time?

    5:18

3. ___Mia___ started ___Swiming___ at 10:45 a.m. and finished at 11:18 a.m. How much time was spent on it?

    33 mins because 45+33=78
    78 mins= 1 hour 18 mins — 11:18   10:00+ 1 hour 18 mi

4. ___Dana~~Ruth~~___ started ___class___ at 3:30 p.m and took 45 minutes to complete it. What was the finish time?

    4:15   30 min +45 mins =75 mins = 1 hour 15 mins

    1 hour 15 mins + 3:00 = 4:15

iM KH

Section C Summary

In this section, we learned to tell and write time to the nearest minute. We solved addition and subtraction problems about time.

the time Han got on the bus:

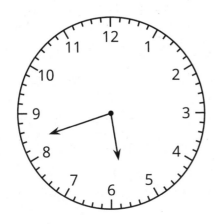

the time Han got off the bus:

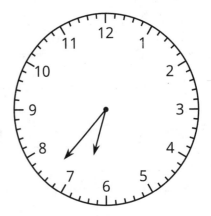

Here is one way to find out how much time Han spent on the bus:

- Count up 3 minutes from 5:42 to 5:45, and then 15 minutes from 5:45 to 6:00.

- Count up 30 minutes from 6:00 to 6:30, and then 7 more minutes to 6:37.

- Add the minutes, $3 + 15 + 30 + 7$, to get 55.

Section C Practice Problems

1. a. Han drew this clock and says it shows 2:16 p.m. Do you agree with Han? Explain your reasoning.

_____

_____

_____

_____

b. Draw the hands on this clock to show 5:55 p.m.

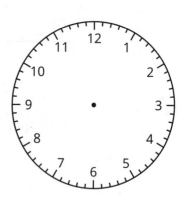

(From Unit 6, Lesson 9.)

2. Mai left to walk the dog at 6:50 a.m. and she returned at 7:44 a.m. How much time did Mai spend walking the dog?

(From Unit 6, Lesson 10.)

iM KH

3. Andre started soccer practice at 3:45 p.m. He left school 75 minutes earlier.

   a. Show the time Andre left school on the clock.

   b. Andre was at soccer practice for 110 minutes. What time did soccer practice end? Explain or show your reasoning.

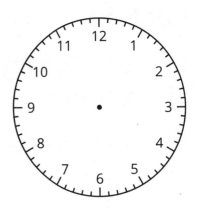

(From Unit 6, Lesson 11.)

4. **Exploration**

   a. What time do you usually go to bed at night?

   b. What time do you usually get up in the morning?

   c. How many minutes do you spend in bed? Explain or show your reasoning.

5. **Exploration**

Priya drew this clockface to show 3:15.

Do you think Priya's clock face is accurate? Explain or show your reasoning.

Section D: Measurement Problems in Context

Lesson 12: Ways to Represent Measurement Situations

- Let's make sense of and represent measurement situations at the fair.

Warm-up: Notice and Wonder: The Fair

What do you notice? What do you wonder?

iM KH

12.1: Giant Pumpkin Event

1. Write a list of mathematical questions that could be asked about this image.

_____

_____

_____

_____

2. Work with your partner to solve the problem you were given by your teacher and show your thinking on a poster. Be sure to write down on your poster the problem you are solving.

12.2: Card Sort: Giant Pumpkins

Your teacher will give you a set of cards with descriptions and diagrams.

Match each description with a diagram that represents the same situation.

Giant Pumpkins

A. Giant pumpkins grow from seedlings. A farmer used 84 liters to water their seedlings with 12 liters each. How many seedlings were there?

Giant Pumpkins

B.

337	84

?

Giant Pumpkins

C.

7	

84

Giant Pumpkins

D. One farmer says he used 337 liters per day to water his giant pumpkin. Another farmer used 84 liters less per day. How much water did she use a day?

Giant Pumpkins

E. A father and a daughter use 337 liters per day to water their pumpkin and 84 liters a day to water their watermelon. How much water do they use all together per day?

Giant Pumpkins

F.

12	

84

Giant Pumpkins

G.

?	84

337

Giant Pumpkins

H. A giant pumpkin gained 12 kilograms per day for 7 days. How much weight did the pumpkin gain during that week?

Giant Pumpkins

I. A pack of giant pumpkin seeds weighs 7 grams. A farmer has 84 grams of seeds. How many packs does she have?

Giant Pumpkins

J.

12	12	12	12	12	12	12

?

Lesson 13: Problems with Missing Information

- Let's find out what information is needed to solve problems about measurements at the fair.

Warm-up: Estimation Exploration: Giant Cantaloupe

A regular cantaloupe weighs between 1 and 5 kilograms.

This cantaloupe melon was a winner at the 2010 Alaska State Fair. How many kilograms do you think it weighs?

Record an estimate that is:

too low	about right	too high

13.1: Info Gap: Pumpkin Weigh-Off

Your teacher will give you either a problem card or a data card. Do not show or read your card to your partner.

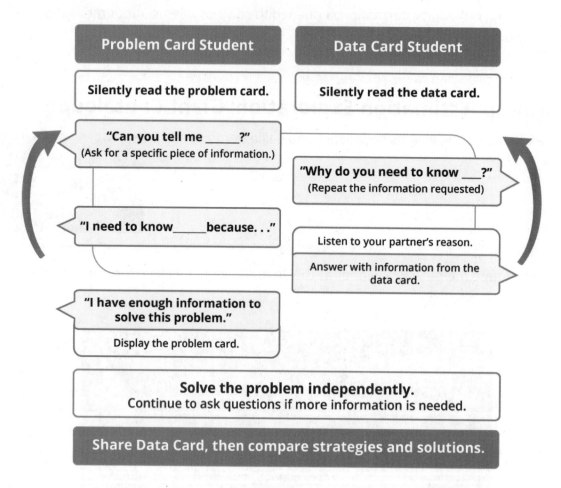

Pause here so your teacher can review your work.

Ask your teacher for a new set of cards and repeat the activity, trading roles with your partner.

iM KH

13.2: Info Gap: Pig Weigh-Off

Your teacher will give you a new problem card or data card. Do not show or read your card to your partner.

Use the same information gap routine to solve the problem. Then, pause so your teacher can review your work.

Ask your teacher for a new set of cards and repeat the activity, trading roles with your partner.

Lesson 14: What Makes Sense in the Problem?

- Let's think about what numbers and questions make sense in problems.

Warm-up: Number Talk: Give and Take

Find the value of each expression mentally.

- $306 + 199$

- $318 + 297$

- $275 + 325$

- $275 + 329$

iM KH

14.1: Carnival Time Number Choice

Here are three problems about time at the carnival. They are missing some information.

1. In the blanks, write numbers or times that make sense for the situation in the problem assigned to you.

    a. Clare waited for Tyler to ride the Ferris wheel. Tyler left at
       _____ and got back at _____. How long did
       Clare wait for Tyler?

    b. When Tyler got back, he and Clare got in line to ride the roller coaster. They
       waited _____ minutes. At _____, they got on the ride. What
       time did they get in line?

    c. Clare and Tyler got to the carnival at _____. After _____
       minutes, they took a break to buy lemonade. What time did they take their
       lemonade break?

2. Share the numbers and times you chose with your group and explain why they
   make sense.

3. Work with your group to solve each problem. Be prepared to explain your
   reasoning.

14.2: Lemonade Break

A lemonade stand at the fair makes 132 liters of lemonade a day. When Clare and Tyler stopped by the stand, there were 90 liters left.

At the end of the day, there were 56 liters of lemonade left, which the vendor put on sale in 4-liter jugs.

Use the information about the lemonade stand to write a question that could be answered with the mathematical work shown.

1. $132 - 90 = 42$

   Question:

   _____

   _____

2.

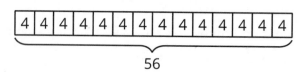

   56

   Question:

   _____

   _____

iM KH

Lesson 15: Ways to Solve Problems and Show Solutions

- Let's solve problems about spending a day at the fair and think about how to best show our solutions.

Warm-up: Number Talk: Divide by 8

Find the value of each expression mentally.

- $80 \div 8$

- $72 \div 8$

- $96 \div 8$

- $96 \div 4$

15.1: A Day at the Fair

You spent a day at the fair. Solve four problems about your day and create a poster to show your reasoning and solutions.

1. You arrived at the fair!

   Entry to the fair is $9 a person. You went there with 6 other people. How much did it cost your group to enter the fair?

2. How did you start your day? (Choose one.)

   You arrived at the giant pumpkin weigh-off at 11:12 a.m. and left at 12:25 p.m. How long were you there?

   You spent 48 minutes at the carnival and left at 12:10 p.m. What time did you get to the carnival?

3. What was next? (Choose one.)

   You visited a barn with 7 sheep. The sheep drink 91 liters of water a day, each sheep drinking about the same amount. How much does each sheep drink a day?

   You visited a life-size sculpture of a cow made of butter. The butter cow weighs 273 kilograms, which is 277 kilograms less than the actual cow. How much does the actual cow weigh?

   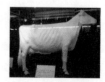

4. Before you went home . . .

   You stopped for some grilled corn on the cob. On the grill, there were 54 ears of corn arranged in 9 equal rows. How many ears of corn were in each row?

iM KH

15.2: A Day at the Fair Gallery Walk

As you visit the posters with your partner:

1. Look for a problem that was solved using a strategy that is different from yours. What made it different? Describe the strategy.

2. Look for ways that your classmates made their thinking and the math work clear to you. Describe at least three things they did or showed on the posters.

_____

_____

_____

_____

Section D Summary

In this section, we solved all kinds of problems about time, weight, and liquid volume. We did so using addition, subtraction, multiplication, and division, as well as different reasoning strategies.

Clare spent 48 minutes at the carnival. She left the carnival at 12:10 p.m. What time did she get to the carnival?

$$11:22 \xleftarrow{-8} 11:30 \xleftarrow{-30} 12:00 \xleftarrow{-10} 12:10$$

A cow made of butter weighs 273 kilograms. That is 277 kilograms less that the actual cow. How much does the actual cow weigh?

```
    1  1
    2  7  3
 +  2  7  7
 ─────────
    5  5  0
```

A grower used 84 liters to water their pumpkin seedlings. Each seedling gets 12 liters. How many seedlings were there?

Lesson 16: Design a Carnival Game

- Let's design a carnival game.

Warm-up: Notice and Wonder: Carnival Games

What do you notice? What do you wonder?

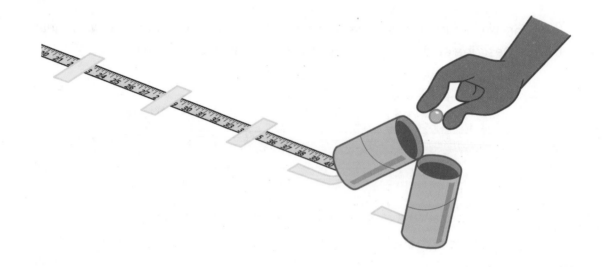

iM KH

16.1: Create Your Own Carnival Game

1. Use the materials to design your own carnival game.

   a. What are the rules of your game?

   b. How does someone win the game?

2. Test out your game at least one time.

3. Redesign your game to include at least 2 of the following:

   ○ length or distance measurement in inches
   ○ time that has passed
   ○ multiplication and division within 100
   ○ addition and subtraction within 1,000

If you have time, play the new and improved game.

Section D Practice Problems

1. Lin's class got 8 pumpkins for a pumpkin carving contest. Each pumpkin weighed 12 pounds.

    a. Which tape diagram represents the situation?

    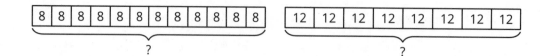

    b. How many pounds did the pumpkins weigh altogether? Explain or show your reasoning.

    (From Unit 6, Lesson 12.)

2. A family brought two pigs to the fair. The first pig weighed 153 kg. The second pig weighed 66 kg less. How much did the second pig weigh?

    (From Unit 6, Lesson 13.)

3. One day, a lemonade stand at the fair sold 56 liters of lemonade in 4-liter packs. How many 4-liter packs did they sell?

    (From Unit 6, Lesson 14.)

iM KH

4. Jada arrived at the fair at 10:15 a.m. She left the fair at 11:47 a.m. How many minutes did Jada spend at the fair? Explain or show your reasoning.

(From Unit 6, Lesson 15.)

5. **Exploration**

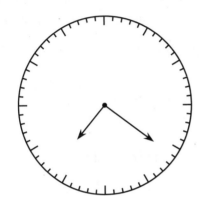

Jada sees this image of a clock in a mirror. What time is it? Explain your reasoning.

_____

_____

6. **Exploration**

Three pumpkins at the fair weigh a total of 1,000 kg.

a. What is one possibility for the 3 pumpkin weights?

b. The lightest of the 3 pumpkins is 255 kg. What is a possibility now for the 3 pumpkin weights?

c. The heaviest of the 3 pumpkins is 428 kg. How much does the 3rd pumpkin weigh?

Glossary

algorithm
A set of steps that works every time as long as the steps are carried out correctly.

area
The number of square units that cover a flat figure without gaps or overlaps.

array
An arrangement of objects in rows and columns. Each column must contain the same number of objects as the other columns, and each row must have the same number of objects as the other rows.

bar graph
A way to show how many in each group or category using the length of rectangles.

denominator
The bottom part of a fraction that tells how many equal parts the whole was partitioned into.

division
Finding the number of groups or finding the size of each group when we share into groups of equal size.

divisor
The number we are dividing by which can represent the size of the groups or the number of groups.

equation
A statement that includes an equal sign (=). It tells us that what is on one side of the sign is equal to what is on the other side.

equivalent fractions
Fractions that have the same size and describe the same point on the number line. For example, $\frac{1}{2}$ and $\frac{2}{4}$ are equivalent fractions.

expanded form
A specific way of writing a number as a sum of hundreds, tens, and ones.

Expanded form writes a number as a sum of the value of each digit. Example: 482 written in expanded form is $400 + 80 + 2$.

expression
An expression has at least 2 numbers and at least one math operation (such as addition, subtraction, multiplication and division).

factor
When we multiply two whole numbers to get a product, each of those numbers is a factor of the product.

fraction
A number used to describe the parts of a whole that has been partitioned into equal parts.

gram
A weight unit that is part of the metric measurement system.

There are 1,000 grams in a kilogram.

key
The part of a picture graph that tells what each picture represents.

kilogram
A weight unit that is part of the metric measurement system.

There are 1,000 grams in a kilogram.

liquid volume
The amount of space that a liquid takes up.

liter
A liquid volume unit that is part of the metric measurement system.

mixed number
A number expressed as a whole number and a fraction less than 1.

multiplication
The operation that tells you the total number of objects when you have a certain number of equal groups.

numerator
The top part of a fraction that tells how many of the equal parts are being described.

parentheses
Grouping symbols that can be used in expressions or equations, such as:

$(3 \times 5) + (2 \times 5), (24 \div 2) + 5 = 17.$

picture graph
A way to show how many in each group or category using pictures of the objects or symbols.

product
The result of multiplying some numbers.

quotient
The result in a division equation.

rounding
A formal way to say which number a given number is closer to. For example, for 182, the number 180 is the closest multiple of ten and 200 is the closest multiple of a hundred. We can round 182 to 180 (if rounding to the nearest ten) or 200 (if rounding to the nearest hundred).

scaled bar graph
A bar graph marked in multiples of some number other than 1.

scaled picture graph
A picture graph where each picture represents an amount other than 1.

square centimeter
A square with side lengths of 1 centimeter.

square foot
A square with side lengths of 1 foot.

square inch
A square with side lengths of 1 inch.

square meter
A square with side lengths of 1 meter.

unit fraction
A fraction with 1 in the numerator.

weight
How heavy something is.

iM KH

Attributions

The Common Core State Standards are trademarks of the Common Core State Standards Initiative. © Copyright 2010. National Governors Association Center for Best Practices and Council of Chief State School Officers. All rights reserved. http://www.corestandards.org/

"Notice and Wonder" and "I Notice/I Wonder" are trademarks of the National Council of Teachers of Mathematics, reflecting approaches developed by the Math Forum (http://www.nctm.org/noticeandwonder/), and used here with permission.

Images that are not the original work of Illustrative Mathematics are in the public domain or released under a Creative Commons Attribution (CC-BY) license, and include an appropriate citation. Images that are the original work of Illustrative Mathematics do not include such a citation.

Image Attributions

Pilolo game, by Benebiankie. CC0. Wikimedia Commons. https://commons.wikimedia.org/wiki/File:Pilolo_game_03.jpg.

By Michael Schwarzenberger. Pixabay. Pixabay. Adapted from https://pixabay.com/photos/biological-leaf-leaves-181237/.

American Bird Grasshopper (cm), by Tom Friedel. CC BY 3.0. Wikipedia. Adapted from https://en.wikipedia.org/wiki/Grasshopper#/media/File:American_Bird_Grasshopper.jpg.

Birch Twigs, by MJ. CC BY-SA 4.0. Wikimedia Commons. https://commons.wikimedia.org/wiki/File:Birch_twigs.jpg.

By terimakasih0. Pixabay. Pixabay. https://pixabay.com/photos/woman-food-stall-fruits-thailand-981797/.

By Jess Bailey Designs. Pexel License. Pexels. https://www.pexels.com/photo/paper-clips-on-white-surface-760897/.

By Pixabay. Pexel License. Pexels. https://www.pexels.com/photo/apples-basket-blur-close-up-533317/.

By Vantage Point Graphics. Pixabay. Pixabay. https://pixabay.com/photos/guinea-pig-cavy-pet-guinea-rodent-242520/.

By skeeze. Pixabay. Pixabay. https://pixabay.com/photos/
yellow-labrador-retriever-golden-742085/.

By Rebecca Lehman. Pixabay. Pixabay. https://pixabay.com/photos/
beta-fish-betta-animal-aquatic-2868325/.

By Tomas Andreopoulos. Pexel License. Pexels. https://www.pexels.com/photo/
adult-brown-tabby-cat-747795/.

By Pixabay. Pexel License. Pexels. https://www.pexels.com/photo/
apartment-bath-bathroom-bathtub-358592/.

By balog. Pixabay. Pixabay. https://pixabay.com/photos/
sink-kitchen-faucet-stainless-208143/.

By Eias Gayles. CC BY 2.0. Flickr. https://www.flickr.com/photos/elias_daniel/281970867.

By Holger Schué. Pixabay. Pixabay. https://pixabay.com/photos/
pot-boiling-water-hot-water-883036/.

By Titanas. CC BY-SA 2.0. Flickr. https://www.flickr.com/photos/titanas/3576536370.

Puyallup Fair, by Chase N. CC BY-SA 2.0. Creative Commons.
https://search.creativecommons.org/photos/dcc14892-9b77-4bdc-8640-da546334ad1e.

Auburn Community Festival 2008, by aresauburn™. CC BY-SA 2.0. Creative Commons.
https://search.creativecommons.org/photos/6f11f3bc-0b4b-4914-b69d-037e9a716655.

By Eric Sonstroem. CC BY-SA 2.0. Creative Commons.
https://search.creativecommons.org/photos/1c48f91d-57a7-4f9b-a440-fc7aed716556.

Giant Pumpkin Festival 10.20.07 111, by Nick Ares. CC BY-SA 2.0. Flickr.
https://www.flickr.com/photos/aresauburnphotos/1667303550/in/photolist.

By PublicDomainImages. Pixabay. Pixabay. https://pixabay.com/photos/
muskmelons-cantaloupes-fruit-melon-387466/.

Giant Cantaloupe, by Jay Galvin. CC BY 2.0. Wikipedia. https://commons.wikimedia.org/
wiki/File:Heavy-lift_melon.jpg.

Fort Edmonton park, by Jason Woodhead. CC BY 2.0. Creative Commons.
https://search.creativecommons.org/photos/f14d1884-d34e-460a-9240-da6d739e13f5.

Lemonade Stand, by Corey Coyle. CC BY 3.0. Wikimedia Commons.

https://commons.wikimedia.org/wiki/File:Lemonade_Stand_-_panoramio_(2).jpg.

Auburn Community Festival 2008, by aresauburn™ . CC BY-SA 2.0. Creative Commons. https://search.creativecommons.org/photos/6d9f09e7-cc61-48b8-b905-d28d9c3a4cc5.

Sheep at a Fair, by Steven Walling. CC BY 3.0. Wikipedia. https://commons.wikimedia.org/wiki/File:Romney_Clark_County_Fair.JPG.

Butter Cow, by Bradley Newman. CC BY-SA 2.0. Creative Commons. https://search.creativecommons.org/photos/6e5e5921-43ff-45af-8698-946d02b51c35.

By pxhere. CC0. pxhere. https://pxhere.com/en/photo/115776.

Notes

Notes

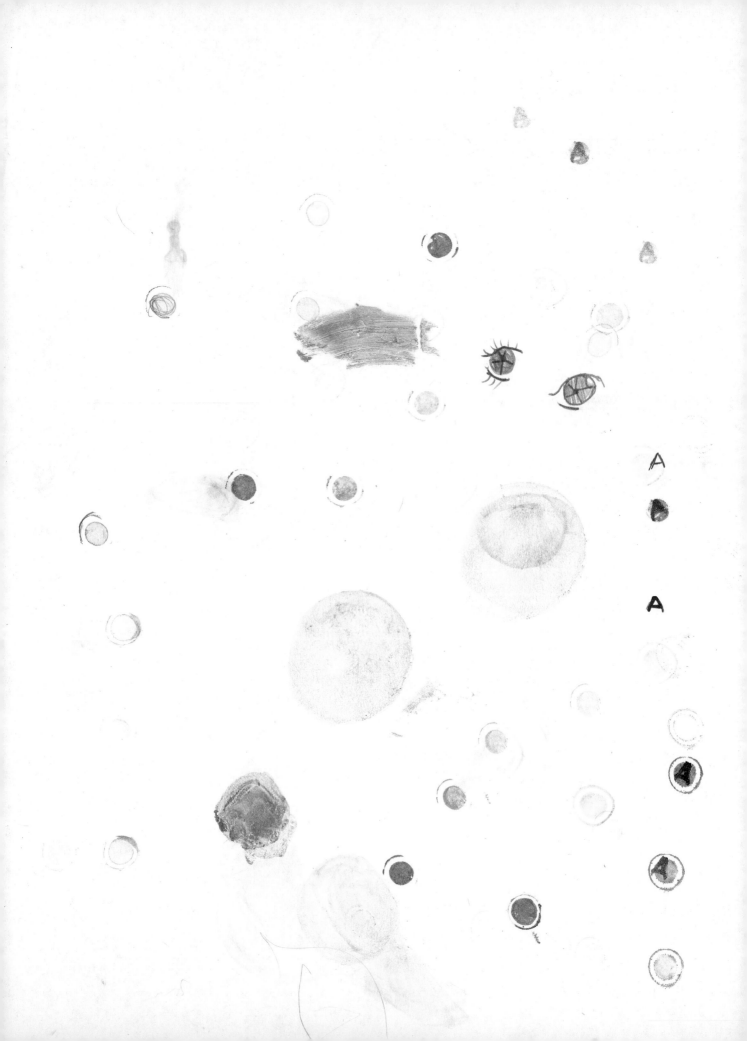

You are
my Mommy

Hi

Hi Sruthi

Hi

hi ★

Sruthi
Your Not
my mom
Jk
you
are